THE  TIMES
GUIDE TO ENGLISH STYLE AND USAGE

Compiled by Tim Austin

TIMES BOOKS
London

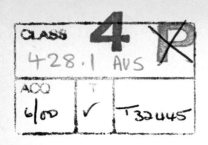
Published by
Times Books
HarperCollins*Publishers*
77-85 Fulham Palace Road
Hammersmith
London W6 8JB

**British Library Cataloguing
in Publication Data**
A catalogue record for this title is
available from the British Library

Compiled and edited by Tim Austin

Printed and bound in Great Britain by
Caledonian

ISBN   0 7230 1045 5

Contents...

This Style Guide aimed originally to provide writers and sub-editors on *The Times* with a quick reference to contentious points of grammar and spelling, to proper names, and to specialised usage which can cause confusion.

The book is intended as a guide, not a straitjacket. Some spellings or constructions are a matter of choice for *The Times*: the rejected usages are not necessarily wrong.

In publishing this guide for a wider audience, I hope that our readers and others will find it an accessible book of reference.

Peter Stothard
September 1999

A...

a, an use *a* before all words beginning with a vowel or diphthong with the sound of *u* (as in *unit*) – *a eulogy, a European* etc; but use *an* before unaspirated *h* – *an heir, an honest woman, an honour*; also, prefer *an hotel, an historic,* and *an heroic*

abattoir

Abbey National (bank, not building society); others with similarly changed status include the Halifax, the Woolwich, the Alliance & Leicester etc. See **building societies**

abbreviations prefer not to abbreviate Professor to Prof, Father to Fr etc; see **military ranks**

abbreviated negatives (can't, don't, shan't etc, plus similar abbreviations such as I'll, you're) should be discouraged in all text except in direct quotes, though they are permissible when the full form would sound pedantic

Abdication cap with specific reference to Edward VIII's; in general sense, use l/c. See **Royal Family**

Aboriginal (native Australian) singular noun and adjective; for plural use *Aborigines*; note l/c *aboriginal* for wider adjectival use

Acas the Advisory, Conciliation and Arbitration Service

accents give French, Spanish, Portuguese, German, Italian and Ancient Greek words their proper accents and diacritical marks; omit in other languages unless you are sure of them. Accents are not necessary in headlines. There is no need for accents in foreign words that have become Anglicised (*hotel, depot, debacle, elite, regime* etc), but keep the accent when it makes a crucial difference to pronunciation – *café, communiqué, fête, fiancée, mêlée, émigré, protégé*; also note *vis-à-vis, façade*. See **foreign words**

Achilles' heel

acknowledgement

acoustic(s) (not accoustic)

Act and **Bill** cap whether fully identified or not

actor, actress see **feminine designations**

Actuary the *Government Actuary* takes caps

AD, BC note that AD comes before the date, eg, *AD35*; BC comes after, eg, *350BC*. With century, both are used after, eg, *3rd century BC/AD*

adapter (person who adapts); *adaptor* (plug, device)

Addenbrooke's Hospital, Cambridge

addresses no commas in *1 Virginia Street* etc; and do not abbreviate *Street*. See **postal addresses**

adidas note l/c

adjectives avoid clichéd adjectives as in *long-felt* want, *serious* danger, *widespread* concern, *substantial* majority etc

Adjutant-General takes the hyphen

Administration (US)

Admiral do not abbreviate to *Adm Jones* etc except in lists; on subsequent mentions, use *the admiral*. See **Armed Forces** special section (page 164)

admissible, inadmissible (not -able)

ad nauseam (not ad nauseum)

adrenalin prefer to adrenaline

adverbs when they are used to qualify adjectives, the joining hyphen is rarely needed, eg, heavily pregnant, classically carved, colourfully decorated. But in some cases, such as well-founded, ill-educated, a hyphen makes the sense clearer. The best guidance is to use the hyphen in these phrases as little as possible or when the phrase would otherwise be ambiguous

adviser (never advisor)

Afrikaans (language) note *Afrikaners* (the people)

affect, effect as a verb, *to affect* means to produce an effect on, to touch the feelings of, or to pretend to have or feel (as in affectation); *to effect* is to bring about, to accomplish

Afghan (noun or adjective); an *afghani* (l/c) is a unit of currency, not a person

after almost invariably to be used rather than *following*. Also, beware of careless use in sentences such as "The British player won a place in the final after beating the seeded German". Instead use "... by beating the seeded German". See **as, following**

afterlife one word

ages normal style is *Joe Brown, 33, a porter*; keep children's ages in this format as figure for the sake of consistency, eg, "Emma Watson, 7, who. . ."; but "the seven-year-old child said . . ." (up to and including ten); occasional variations such as "Andrew Hunt, who is 74, said. . ." are also permissible. Note caps in *Ice Age, Stone Age, the Dark Ages* etc

ageing note the middle *e* – as in *axeing, likeable, mileage, moveable, rateable, sizeable, unlikeable, unshakeable* etc. Common exceptions are listed separately, eg, see **unmistakable**

aggravate means to make (an evil or complaint) worse. It does not mean to annoy or irritate

AGM caps, but prefer *annual meeting* in text

agoraphobia (not agaro-, agra- etc)

Aids short for acquired immune deficiency syndrome (not auto-immune etc); it is not a disease, but a medical condition. Diseases that affect people who are HIV-positive may be called Aids-related diseases; although prefer not to use the phrase "died of Aids", it is now permissible in standfirsts, headings etc. See **HIV**

AIM the Alternative Investment Market; keep caps in abbreviation

Air Accidents Investigation Branch caps; note *Accidents*

airbase, airstrip, airspace no hyphens; but see **air fares, air show, airstrikes**

air-conditioner, air-conditioning (hyphenate)

aircraft try to avoid *planes* in text, though *planes* would be acceptable in headlines. Even there, *jets* (where applicable – remember that some aircraft are still turbo-prop) or *aircraft* would be better. See **planes**

aircraft names are italicised, as with ships' or locomotive names, eg, the *Enola Gay* (Hiroshima bomber). See **locomotive, ships**

aircraft types no hyphens between letter and numbers, eg, B52, F111 etc

aircraftman, aircraftwoman (not aircraftsman etc); see **Armed Forces** special section (page 164)

air fares two words, as *rail fares, bus fares* etc

air force cap in full name such as Royal Air Force (thereafter the

RAF), US Air Force (USAF), Brazilian Air Force (thereafter the air force, l/c); and l/c in adjectival use, eg, *an air force raid*. See **Armed Forces** special section (page 164)

Air Miles take care when to cap: the Air Miles scheme is run by BA and should usually be capped; but use l/c in a general context

airports as a general rule for British airports, use the name of the city or town followed by l/c airport, eg, Manchester airport, Leeds/Bradford airport, East Midlands airport, Luton airport; but see **Heathrow, Gatwick, Stansted**

air raid two words, but see **airstrikes**

air show two words; cap when specific, eg, the Paris Air Show, the Farnborough Air Show

airstrikes one word in military sense, but see **air raid**

akimbo use only with reference to arms (never legs). It means hands on the hips with elbows turned outwards

al- as the prefix to Arabic nouns (including names), prefer *al-* to the *el-* form, except where *el-* has become widely accepted

Albert Hall generally omit Royal

A level, O level hyphenate only when adjectival, eg, A-level results etc. See **examinations**

Al Fayed Mohamed Al Fayed is chairman of Harrods. His youngest brother Ali Fayed is deputy chairman of Harrods. Their brother Saleh Fayed is not a resident of the UK. The brothers should be spelt like this, with no variation. The late elder son was Dodi Fayed

Alfa Romeo

alibi not a general alternative to *excuse*; it means being elsewhere at the material time

Allahu akbar (God is greatest)

allcomers one word

Allende, Isabel, the Chilean novelist (born in Lima, Peru) is the niece and goddaughter of the former Chilean President, Salvador Allende, NOT his daughter

allege avoid the suggestion that the writer is making the allegation, so specify its source. Do not use *alleged* as a synonym of *ostensible, apparent* or *reputed*

All England Club (home of the Wimbledon championships); no hyphen

Allies cap the Allies in the Second World War context; generally, l/c *alliance*, as in the *Atlantic alliance*, *Gulf War alliance* etc

Allitt, Beverly (child-killer convicted in May 1993)

all right (never alright)

All Souls College, Oxford no apostrophe; see **Oxford colleges**

all-time avoid as in *all-time high*; use *highest* instead

alsatian (German shepherd dog); l/c as for other breeds of dogs; but note exceptions such as Yorkshire terrier. See **dogs**

alternative of two things; of three or more, use *choice*

al-Yamamah (oil-for-arms defence project); note l/c and hyphen

Amateur Athletic Association (not Athletics)

Ambassador cap when specific, eg, the French Ambassador, thereafter *the ambassador*

America(n)/US in general, use American as in "American cities, American food" etc; but use US in headlines and in the context of government institutions, such as US Congress, US Navy, US military operation. Never use *America* when ambiguity could occur with Canada or Latin America. See **United States**

American spellings normally use the English spelling even with offices or institutions such as Secretary of Defense (change to *Defence*), American Federation of Labor (change to *Labour*), or with buildings, eg, the Lincoln Center (change to *Centre*); but *Labor Day* (which has no UK equivalent) is an exception; see also **Pearl Harbor**

America's Cup, the (yachting)

amid (not amidst); similarly *among*, not amongst

amok (not amock or amuck)

amphitheatres in classical context these are oval or circular (eg, the Colosseum in Rome); do not confuse with theatres which are semi-circular or horseshoe-shaped

Amsterdam treaty l/c *t*, but note caps for the Treaty of Amsterdam. See **Maastricht**

analog (in computer context); but use *analogue* as in an analogous or parallel thing. See **program**

ancestor strictly means a person from whom another is directly descended, especially someone more distant than a grandparent. Do not use in the looser sense of *predecessor*; eg, Queen Elizabeth I is not the *ancestor* of the present Queen

Ancient Briton/Britain note also Ancient Greek/Greece, Ancient Egyptian/Egypt, Ancient Roman/Rome

Andersen, Hans Christian (not Anderson)

aneurysm (not aneurism)

Anglicise, Anglophile caps, note l/c *anglophone*

Anglo-Irish agreement See **Ireland**

angst roman l/c

animals beware the solecism "birds and animals"; use *birds and mammals* instead

animal names call an animal "he" or "she" if the sex is definitely known or if called by a masculine or feminine name (eg, Felix the cat had only himself to blame). But use "it" if the sex is unspecified. On the racing pages, horses are always "he" or "she"

annexe (noun), but to *annex* (verb)

anoint (not annoint)

answerphone or use *answering machine*

Antarctic, Arctic (never Antartic etc)

antennae plural of *antenna* in zoological sense; use *antennas* in radio or aerial sense

Antichrist (initial cap)

anticipate do not use for *expect*. It means to deal with, or use, in advance of, or before, the due time. To anticipate marriage is different from expecting to marry

antidepressant noun or adjective, no hyphen

anti-Semitic, anti-Semitism

antisocial, anticlimax

Anti-Terrorist Branch, Special Branch note caps; but police squads in most cases l/c, except *Flying Squad* and *Royalty and Diplomatic Protection Squad*

any more always two words

Apennines, Italy (not Appenines)

apostrophes with proper names/nouns ending in s that are singular, follow the rule of writing what is voiced, eg, *Keats's poetry*, *Sobers's batting*, *The Times's style* (or *Times style*); and with names where the final s is soft, use s', eg, *Rabelais' writings*, *Delors' presidency*; plurals follow normal form, eg, *Lehman Brothers' loss* etc

Note that with Greek names of more than one syllable that end in s, do not use the apostrophe s, eg, *Aristophanes' plays*, *Achilles' heel*, *Archimedes' principle*

Beware of organisations that have variations as their house style, eg, St Thomas' Hospital, where we must respect their whim

Also, take care with apostrophes with plural nouns, eg, *women's*, not womens'; *children's*, not childrens'; *people's*, not peoples'

An apostrophe should be used to indicate the plural of single letters, eg, *p's and q's*

Use the apostrophe in expressions such as *two years' time*, *several hours' delay* etc.

apparatchik

appellations almost every person should be granted the courtesy of a title. The exceptions are convicted offenders, the dead (but not the recently dead, except in obituaries) and cases where common usage omits a title. Sportsmen, artists, authors etc should normally be given a title except where it sounds inappropriate.

General rules:

a. First mention, Herbert Palfry, Juliette Worth, subsequently Mr Palfry, Mrs/Miss/Ms Worth

b. Put the name first, then the age (if relevant), then the description; eg, Jane Fonda, 57, the American actress; avoid the journalese construction "actress Jane Fonda"

c. Avoid initials and middle initials (as in American names) unless the person is best-known thereby (eg, W.G. Grace)

d. Ms is nowadays fully acceptable when a woman wants to be called thus, or when it is not known for certain if she is Mrs or Miss

e. Dr is no longer confined to medical doctors; if a person has a doctorate from a reputable university, Dr is acceptable

f. Court proceedings: accused people should be accorded the appropriate title (Mr, Miss etc) after name and first name have been given at first mention; only convicted persons should be referred to by surname alone

See also **foreign names, titles, Armed Forces** special section (page 164), **Courts** special section (page 176)

appendix plural *appendices*, but note *appendixes* in anatomy

appraise means *evaluate*; do not confuse with *apprise* meaning *inform*

April Fool's Day, April fool, but *All Fools' Day*

Aqaba, Gulf of (Red Sea)

aqueduct (not aquaduct)

Arab use with care

Arabic names use with care; but remember the basic rule of *al-X* (l/c al with hyphen, before name; rarely use the *el-* form); see **al-**

Arafat, Yassir (not Yasser)

arbitrate, arbitration do not confuse with *mediate, mediation*. An *arbitrator* hears evidence from different parties then hands down a decision; a *mediator* listens to the different arguments then tries to bring the parties to agreement

archaeologist, archaeology

archbishops
a. *Anglican archbishops and diocesan bishops*: at first mention, the Archbishop of Barchester, the Most Rev John Smith; or the Bishop of Barchester, the Right Rev John Smith, but if a doctor, the Bishop of Barchester, Dr John Smith; subsequent references, *the archbishop* (*the bishop*), or Dr Smith (if so entitled) – never Mr Smith
b. The Archbishop of Canterbury is Primate of All England, the Archbishop of York is Primate of England
c. Anglican bishops are *consecrated*, Roman Catholic bishops *ordained*
d. *Roman Catholic archbishops and bishops*: at first mention: the Roman Catholic Archbishop of Liverpool, the Most Rev John X; or the Roman Catholic Bishop of Plymouth, the Right Rev Christopher Y; subsequent mentions, Archbishop X (Bishop Y) or *the archbishop* (*the bishop*), or Dr Y (if so entitled). See **Churches** special section (page 172)

Argentine adjective; note an *Argentinian* is a person from Argentina (never the Argentine)

armada be careful with use of this word: it means a fleet of armed ships, so strictly should not be applied to any collection of boats or ships

Armageddon cap

armchair, deckchair no hyphens

Armed Forces, the caps; see also **Services**

Armistice Day not the same as Remembrance Sunday (unless November 11 falls on a Sunday); see **two minutes' silence, Remembrance Sunday**

Army cap in context of the *British Army* (thereafter *the Army*, capped) and foreign armies, as in the *Belgian Army, Iraqi Army* (but thereafter *the army*, l/c); note always l/c when used adjectivally, eg, *an army helicopter*; see **Armed Forces** special section (page 164)

Arran, Isle of (Firth of Clyde); note the *Aran Islands* (one *r*) off Co Galway in western Ireland, *Aran Island* (singular) off Co Donegal and an *Aran sweater* etc

artefact do not use *artifact*

artistic movements cap *Art Deco, Classical, Neo-Classical, Cubist, Gothic, Impressionist, Minimalist, Modernist, Post-Modern, Pre-Columbian, Pre-Raphaelite, Romantic, Surrealist* etc in cultural contexts; but in wider general use, l/c, eg, "He had a surrealist sense of humour but a romantic nature"

as beware of sloppy use in sentences such as "They were moved out as the blast tore open the building"; instead use simply *"after* the blast..."

Asean Association of South East Asian Nations: Indonesia, Singapore, Malaysia, Thailand, the Philippines, Brunei, Vietnam, Burma and Laos. Note that Cambodia is due to join at some unspecified date. See **South-East Asia, Far East**

ASH Action on Smoking and Health; use caps for abbreviation of the anti-smoking pressure group

Asia-Pacific Economic Co-operation forum use *Apec* as abbreviation

assassin, assassination only to be used in the murder of a statesman or politician from a political motive; not to be used for the killing of general celebrities or others. See **execution, killer**

Assisted Places Scheme caps, but *assisted places* (in schools)

assizes like quarter sessions, no longer function, having been replaced by Crown Courts. See **quarter sessions**

Association of First Division Civil Servants use *First Division Association* for short

assure you *assure* your life; *ensure* means to make certain; you *insure* against risk

asylum-seekers hyphenate

at the present time, at this time use *now*; but avoid the phrase *as of now*

Athenaeum, the see **London clubs**

Atlantic (Ocean), North Atlantic, South Atlantic see **transatlantic**

Atomic Energy Authority, UK (not Agency); abbreviated to AEA; but note *International Atomic Energy Agency*, abbreviated to IAEA

Attorney-General, Solicitor-General (law officers, not legal officers); hyphenate both; see **Courts** special section (page 176)

Auditor-General hyphenate

Auntie (not aunty) as colloquialism for the BBC. See **BBC**

Autocue proprietary term, so cap

Autumn Statement (caps); see **Budget**

Awol (not AWOL) absent without leave

AXA League (Sunday cricket league); note also the *Benson and Hedges Cup*. See **Sports** special section (page 185)

axeing note middle *e*; but try to avoid in sense of *cutting jobs, dismissal* etc

ay (yes), *aye* (ever), *Ayes* (debate)

Ayckbourn, Alan

B...

BAA (airports operator); no longer British Airports Authority

Baath party (not Ba'ath)

baby-walker

baccalaureate use Anglicised spelling with l/c for general use, but cap in specific context of the *International Baccalaureate*; and note the specifically French examination or degree, the *Baccalauréat* (italic, cap, accent, no final "e")

Bacharach, Burt

B&B (abbreviation for bed and breakfast); use caps and close up around ampersand

back benches (parliamentary); two words, but note *backbenchers*, *backbench* (adjective, as in *backbench revolt*). See **Politics** special section (page 179)

back burner (no hyphen), but be sparing of the cliché "on the back burner"

backlash overworked word; always try to avoid

backstreet(s) noun or adjective, no hyphen; similarly, *backyard*

"back to basics" use in quotes, no hyphen

bacteria note the term is not interchangeable with viruses. Note that antibiotics are used to treat bacterial but not viral infections. See **medical terms, meningitis**

bail out (as in to *bail someone out of trouble*); note also *to bail water from a boat*, but *to* **bale out** *of an aircraft* (to escape); and *bailout*

balk (not baulk)

ball plural in Court Page headlines is *dances*

ballets use italics for titles; see **Arts** special section (page 169)

ballgown one word

balloted like *benefited*, *budgeted* etc, has only one *t*

Balpa British Air Line Pilots' Association

banister (not bannister)

Bank Holiday also *Bank Holiday Monday* etc

bankruptcy in Britain people *file a petition for bankruptcy*; they do not *file for bankruptcy*

Bar, the (legal); also cap for the *Bar of the House of Commons*. See **Courts** special section (page 176) and **Politics** special section (page 179)

barbecue, barbecuing

Bar school l/c *s*, as this is not its official title, and no longer Bar law school. Its full name is the *Inns of Court School of Law*

Barnardo's (no longer Dr Barnardo's Homes)

Bart's abbreviation of St Bartholomew's Hospital, London

Basle, Switzerland (not Basel); see **Berne**

basically greatly overworked word which rarely adds anything to a sentence. Always try to avoid

basis *on a . . . basis* is a cliché and should be avoided; for *employment on a part-time basis* use *part-time employment*

battalion (not batallion). Write *1st Battalion, 7th Battalion* etc (not First, Seventh). See **Armed Forces** special section (page 164)

Battersea Dogs' Home (formal title is *The Dogs' Home, Battersea,* but not usually necessary to spell it out)

battle avoid using as a transitive verb as in "The students battled the police. . ."; use *fought* or *battled against* instead

BBC no need to spell out as British Broadcasting Corporation, though *the corporation* is a useful alternative in text. Note BBC Television, BBC1, BBC2, and BBC Radio (caps). Note also *Chairman of the (Board of) Governors* takes caps (although chairman in most other cases is l/c). This is because we cap the *Director-General* and when both appear in the same story it is anomalous to cap the one and not the other. Cap *the BBC Board of Governors,* but l/c *the governors* at other mentions. See **radio, television**

BBC Charter cap when in full, l/c for *charter* on subsequent mentions

BC see **AD**

Beatles, the no need to cap *the* unless at the start of a sentence; similarly *the Rolling Stones* and *the Manic Street Preachers* etc, but prefer to keep cap T with *The Who* and *The The*

Becket note *à* with St Thomas à Becket

Beduin plural; the singular is *Bedu*

Beethoven, Ludwig van (not von); normally Beethoven will suffice; see **Van**

beg the question do not confuse with *ask the question*. To beg a question is to *evade* it

Beijing (no longer Peking); see **Chinese names**

Belarus (no longer Belorussia)

beleaguered rapidly becoming a cliché, especially in a political context, so best avoided

Belfast see **Ireland**

bellringer, bellringing, belltower no hyphens. See **peal**

benchmark (no hyphen)

benefited

benzene (substance obtained from coal-tar); note *benzine*, a spirit obtained from petroleum

-berg, -burg always check spelling of towns with these endings, and those ending in *-burgh*, *-borough*, *-brough*

Berkeley Square, West End of London; similarly, Berkeley, California

Bermudian (not Bermudan); but note a *Bermuda-rigged boat*

Berne, Switzerland (not Bern)

berserk (not beserk)

BEST Investment (no longer BESt)

bestseller, bestselling one word

bête noire note italics and final *e*

Betjeman, Sir John (not Betjamin)

Bevan, Aneurin, but **Ernest Bevin**

Beverly Hills

Bhutto, Benazir use Miss rather than Ms or Mrs on subsequent mentions

bi- take care with this difficult prefix. Its correct use is in Latin compounds, where it has the force of two, not half, such as *bicentenary/bicentennial* (a two-hundredth anniversary), or *biennial* (recurring every two years). *Biannual* means twice a year; to avoid confusion, use *twice a year*

biased

Bible cap and roman, not italic, but note l/c *biblical*; for biblical references: II Corinthians ii, 2; Luke iv, 5. Note *Bible Belt*. See **Churches** special section (page 172)

bid do not use in text as synonym of *effort, attempt* or *try*, though it may be used sparingly in headlines in this context

bight (curve in a coastline or river); do not confuse with *bite* involving teeth. See **bite, German Bight**

Bill and **Act** caps whether fully identified or not

Bill of Rights cap even when non-specific, eg, "If the Government were to introduce a Bill of Rights. . ."

billion (one thousand million, not a million million). Write £5 billion, £15 billion (£5bn, £15bn in headlines), three billion, 15 billion etc. See **millions, trillion**

biological terms see **scientific names**

Biro trade name, so cap; alternative is *ballpoint pen*

birthday people and animals have *birthdays*; everything else has *anniversaries*. Better to write *33rd birthday, 65th birthday* etc (any number higher than tenth), despite the usual rules on spelling out ordinals. See **numbers**

birthrate, birthright, birthplace no hyphens, but note *birth control, birth certificate* etc

bisexual pronouns *he* and *his* can no longer refer to both sexes equally; *he or she* will sometimes do. Always be sensitive in this contentious area

bishops see **archbishops**

Bishopsgate, City of London (not Bishopgate)

Bishop's Stortford

bite (as with teeth) do not confuse with the computing term *byte* or the geographical *bight*. See **bight, byte, soundbite**

blacklist one word as noun or verb; see **shortlist**

blackout noun, one word

blacks (people), l/c; do not use *non-whites* and be sensitive to local usage, eg, *African-American* is now often used in the United States. See **Coloureds, race**

blackspot (accident, unemployment etc), one word; similarly, *troublespot*

blame take care with this word; blame is attached to causes, not effects. So write "Bad weather is blamed for my bronchitis", not "My bronchitis is blamed on bad weather"

bloc use in context such as the *former Soviet bloc*, a *power bloc* etc; but note *block vote*

blond (men), *blonde* (women)

bloodied as in *bloodied but unbowed*; but *red-blooded* etc

blood sports similarly field sports; see **foxhunt**

Bloomingdale's (New York store)

Blue cap both for an Oxbridge sportsman or woman and for the award itself. See **Sports** special section (page 185)

blue-collar workers similarly *white-collar workers*

blueprint avoid this greatly overworked word when all you mean is *plan*, *scheme* or *proposal*

Boadicea (no longer Boudicca)

boat generally used of a small vessel, including fishing boats up to the size of a trawler; a *ship* is a large seagoing vessel big enough to carry smaller boats. In the Royal Navy, submarines are called boats. All take the pronoun *she* and the possessive *her*. See **ships**

Boat Race (annual Oxford-Cambridge race); use caps

boffin do not use as a synonym of *scientist*, except ironically or in direct quotes

Bogart, Humphrey but note (Sir) Dirk Bogarde

bogey (golf); note also *bogie* (wheels), *bogy* (ghost) and *bogeyman*

Bogotá (capital of Colombia)

Bohemian cap noun, but note l/c adjective *bohemian*

Bolshevik

bombshell avoid metaphorical use, as in cliché *drop a bombshell*

bonanza greatly overworked word that should be avoided wherever possible

Bonhams (auction house); no apostrophe

Boodle's (London club). See **London clubs**

Booth, Cherie Tony Blair's wife should be referred to as Cherie Booth wherever possible; refer to Cherie Blair only in contexts when she is clearly in the role of Prime Minister's wife, eg, at summit meetings or on the campaign trail. In legal contexts, write Cherie Booth, QC, at first mention. Subsequent mentions, Ms Booth

bored with (not *of*)

borstals no longer exist; now known as *young offender institutions*

bortsch (Russian or Polish soup)

Bosphorus

Boutros Boutros Ghali (former UN Secretary-General); no hyphens and at subsequent mentions, Dr Boutros Ghali. His successor is the Ghanaian Kofi Annan

Bowes Lyon no hyphen for most of the family, but always important to check in *Who's Who* or *Debrett*

bow-tie

box office as noun, two words; hyphenate when adjectival, eg, *box-office success*

boyfriend, girlfriend

Boy Scouts now known as *Scouts* in the UK. *Cub Scouts* have replaced Wolf Cubs; *Scoutleaders* have replaced Scoutmasters. Also cap *Scouting* in the context of the movement. In the US they are still known as Boy Scouts. See also **Girl Guides**

braille l/c

brainchild try to avoid this cliché

branch note *Special Branch, Anti-Terrorist Branch* in police context

Brands Hatch

breakout, breakdown one word as noun; but note *to break out* etc, and hyphenated *break-up*

breathtaking no hyphen

Brent Spar is a storage buoy, not an oil platform or rig; note that *oil platforms* stand on the seabed; *oilrigs* are small mobile installations for oil exploration

Bretton Woods (as in world trade)

Breughel (artists)

bridges cap as in Severn Bridge, London Bridge, Southwark Bridge, Golden Gate Bridge

Bridgwater, Somerset (note no middle *e*)

Brink's-Mat

Britain/Great Britain = England, Wales and Scotland. *United Kingdom* = Britain and Northern Ireland. *British Isles* = United Kingdom and the Republic of Ireland, Isle of Man and Channel Islands. Take care with these distinctions

Britannia see **Royal Yacht**

British Athletic Federation (not Athletics)

British Home Stores note the abbreviation Bhs

British Standards Institution (not Institute); abbreviation is BSI. It awards companies, goods etc its *Kitemark* (cap)

Britpop (not Brit Pop)

Brittany Bretagne in French

Broadcasting Standards Commission formed from merged Broadcasting Standards Council and Broadcasting Complaints Commission

Broadmoor inmates are *patients*, not prisoners

broadsheet preferable to *quality* for describing the serious British press

Brookings Institution, Washington (not Institute)

Brooks's (London club). See **London clubs**

Brummie (not Brummy); cap people and dialect, eg, *Geordie, Scouse* etc. See **Cockney**

Brylcreem

BSE bovine spongiform encephalopathy, or "mad cow" disease

BSkyB News International, the subsidiary of The News Corporation that owns *The Times*, owns 40 per cent of BSkyB (British Sky Broadcasting Group Ltd). So BSkyB can be called an associate company of News International, or of News Corp. There is a choice of up to 40 channels available in the UK on the Astra satellite; BSkyB owns 11. See **News International,** *The Times*

BT usual abbreviated form of British Telecommunications plc, but it is often convenient to use British Telecom at first mention, and BT subsequently

Budget cap the *British Budget*, otherwise l/c. Note l/c *d* for *Budget day* and also note *Pre-Budget Report* and *Autumn Statement* (caps)

Buggins's turn (not Buggins')

builder's merchant(s)

building societies cap full name, eg, Skipton Building Society, thereafter *the Skipton*, or *the society* etc. Take care with societies that have become banks. See **Abbey National**

bullion (gold or silver in unminted form)

bull-mastiff, bull-terrier see **dogs**

bullring but the *Bull Ring* in Birmingham

bull's-eye (use hyphen)

bungee (as in jumping)

Bunsen burner

BUPA (no longer Bupa)

Burma (not Myanmar except in direct quotes); the inhabitants are *Burmese*, and note that *Burmans* are a Burmese people

Burnet, (Sir) Alastair

Burns Night (January 25); caps, no apostrophe

burnt (not burned)

Burton upon Trent no hyphens; note l/c for the colloquial *gone for a burton*

bus, buses noun; but in verbal use *busses, bussed, bussing*

Bush, George W. (do not use Jr)

Bushey, Hertfordshire but Bushy Park, near Hampton Court

Bussell, Darcey (ballerina)

buyout, buyback one word; but prefer hyphens for *buy-in, take-off, shake-out, shake-up, sell-off, sell-out* etc

by-election

bylaw

bypass noun or verb

by-product

bystander

byte (computer term for a small collection of bits – binary digits – roughly equivalent to one character); do not confuse with *bite* (as with teeth). But note *soundbite*

Byzantine cap in all contexts

BZW Barclays de Zoete Wedd

C...

cabbie (not cabby) as colloquialism for taxi driver

Cabinet cap in both British and foreign use, whether used as a noun or adjectivally. The only exception is the informal *kitchen cabinet*. Note *Cabinet Office, Cabinet Secretary* (or *Secretary of the Cabinet*). Cabinet committees should be capped, eg, *the Cabinet Committee on Science and Technology*. See **Politics** special section (page 181)

Caernarfon (town and parliamentary constituency, no longer Caernarvon); but note Lord Carnarvon

Caesarean section

café note accent

cagoule but note *kaftan*

call-up noun, but note *to call up*

camaraderie (not cameraderie)

Camborne, Cornwall (not Cambourne)

Cambridge University colleges and halls are: Christ's College; Churchill College; Clare College; Clare Hall; Corpus Christi College; Darwin College; Downing College; Emmanuel College; Fitzwilliam College; Girton College; Gonville and Caius College; Homerton College; Hughes Hall; Jesus College; King's College; Lucy Cavendish College; Magdalene College; New Hall; Newnham College; Pembroke College; Peterhouse; Queens' College; Robinson College; St Catharine's College; St Edmund's College; St John's College; Selwyn College; Sidney Sussex College; Trinity College; Trinity Hall; Wolfson College

camellia (not camelia)

Campbell, Alastair (not Alistair); Tony Blair's press secretary

Camra the Campaign for Real Ale; note l/c

cancer heart disease not cancer is "the biggest killer" in the UK

cannon (military), singular and plural; but note *canons* (both churchmen and church laws) and *canon* as a collection or list of an author

canvas (material, painting); note *canvass* (votes)

Canton now Guangzhou; see **Chinese names**

CAP common agricultural policy; l/c when spelt out in text

Cape Town

capitalisation in general, the proper names of people and places, formal titles or titles of important offices, and the names of well-known and substantial institutions, all require capitals. As a rule of thumb, cap specifics (eg, *the French Foreign Minister*), but l/c non-specifics (eg, *EU foreign ministers*). But some terms, eg, *Act, Bill, Cabinet, Civil Service*, always cap. See **initials**

capsize see **-ise, -isation**

captions when space is tight, just the surname is acceptable, even when the person is titled, eg, Sir Marcus Fox would be simply Fox, as in headlines. Where women are photographed, give the woman's first name and surname where possible.
Identify people in a photograph with *left* and *right* etc, using commas, not parentheses (eg, Fred Smith, left, and his wife leaving the court)

car boot sale no hyphen

carcass

cardholder

Carlos the Jackal no quotes, no commas; always mention his full name, Ilich Ramírez Sánchez

carmaker one word

car park two words, note *multistorey car park*

carpetbagger one word

Carrott, Jasper (not Carrot)

cashcard (in general sense); note also *cashflow, cashback*

Cashpoint Lloyds Bank's cash machine system, so cap and do not use generically; in the general sense, use *cash dispenser* or *cash machine*, or less formally, *hole in the wall*

Castro, President (Fidel) use *Señor* or *the President* after first mention rather than Dr

Catch-22 avoid the grossly overworked cliché *Catch-22 situation*

cathedrals cap when giving the full name, eg, St Paul's Cathedral, Wells Cathedral; similarly the names of churches, eg, St Mary's Church, Ely, unless the church name specifically excludes it, eg, St Stephen's, Ely

Catherine always check the spelling; note a Catherine wheel (firework); St Catharine's College, Cambridge; St Katharine Docks, London

Catholic in church context, use *Roman Catholic* at first mention, then *Catholic*. See **Churches** special section (page 172)

Catmark the new financial products version of the Kitemark; similarly *Cat standard* etc

cat's eyes should preferably be called reflecting roadstuds; *Catseye* is a trademark

caviare (not caviar)

CD-Rom compact disc, read only memory; note CD-i (interactive compact disc system)

ceasefire

Ceausescu, Nicolae (not Ceaucescu)

ceilidh Highland social gathering

Cellophane proprietary term, so cap

celsius, centigrade use either term. In news stories, use both centigrade and fahrenheit, eg, "The temperature rose to 16C (61F)"; do not use degree sign

centenarian see also **septuagenarian, octogenarian, nonagenarian**

centenaries use *centenary, bicentenary, tercentenary*; after that, use *four hundredth anniversary*, etc

Center Parcs

Central Europe note cap C

Central St Martins College of Art and Design no apostrophe in St Martins; use *St Martins* at subsequent mentions

Centre, the use cap in political context of *the Centre*, as with *Left* and *Right*. Similarly, *Centre Left, Centre Right* as nouns, but note l/c for

C

adjectival use, eg, *a centre-left politician, a right-wing policy.* See **Left**, **Right**, **Politics** special section (page 181)

Centre Court see **Wimbledon**

centrepiece no hyphen

centring but note *centering of arches* in bridge-building

centuries write *the 3rd century BC, the 9th century, the 18th century* etc; and hyphenate when used adjectivally, eg, *20th-century architecture*

CERN the European Organisation for Nuclear Research, based in Geneva; note all caps

Ceylon now Sri Lanka. The people are *Sri Lankan*, the majority group are the *Sinhalese*

cha-cha-cha (not cha-cha)

chainsaw one word

chairman still common usage referring to men and women, except in quotes, but *chairwoman* is acceptable. Avoid *chair* and *chairperson* (except in quotes and phrases such as *addressing remarks to the chair*). In most cases, keep *chairman* l/c, but occasionally cap, as with BBC, Bar Council, and US Federal Reserve Board

chamber (of the House of Commons); use l/c. See **Politics** special section (page 181)

champagne note l/c; use only for the product of the Champagne region of France; otherwise use *sparkling wine*. The champagne producers protect their name rigorously. See **wines**

changeable

Changing the Guard (not . . . of the Guard); see **Trooping the Colour**

Channel 4, Channel 5 (not Four, Five); see **television**

Channel Tunnel with cap *T*, but thereafter l/c *tunnel* if the context is clear; note also *Channel Tunnel rail link*. Note that *Le Shuttle* trains are no longer called thus; they are now *Eurotunnel trains*. See **Eurotunnel**

Chanukkah prefer this to variants such as Hanukkah etc, for the Jewish festival of lights

charge that do not use this Americanism as a synonym of *allege that*

charisma find an alternative such as *presence, inspiration* etc for this boring cliché

Charity Commission (not Charities)

Charollais (cattle or sheep)

charters (as in John Major's initiative) see **Citizen's Charter, Parent's Charter, Patient's Charter.** Note also *Charter Mark*

Château-Lafite (not Lafitte); note hyphen

chat show, game show, quiz show, talk show no hyphens; note also *chatline, sexline*

cheap goods are *cheap*, prices are *low*

Chechnya (not Chechenia); note adjective *Chechen*

check-in noun, but note *checklist, checkout counter*

cheerleader one word

Chekhov, Anton

chequebook one word, either as noun or adjective, eg, *chequebook journalism*

chess names note Garry Kasparov, Anatoly Karpov, Judit Polgar. Note also Fide, not FIDE, and l/c *grandmaster*. See **Russian names**

Chester-le-Street

chickenpox no hyphen; similarly *smallpox*

Chief Constable caps when referring to a specific, as in *Chief Constable of Lancashire*; thereafter, *the chief constable*. See **police ranks**

Chief Inspector of Prisons/. . . of Schools note also *Chief Medical Officer*

Chief Whip caps; see **whips**

childcare similarly *healthcare*

ChildLine (charity); note cap *L*

Children Act 1989 (not Children's); note also cap *T* for *The Children's Society*

chimpanzees are apes, not monkeys

Chinese names the Pinyin rather than the traditional Wade-Giles system is now used, so write Beijing, Mao Zedong (though Chairman

Mao or just Mao are acceptable), Zhou Enlai etc. For Chinese place names, follow spellings in *The Times Atlas of the World*: eg, Guangzhou (formerly Canton), Sichuan (formerly Szechuan). See **Peking**

chopper, copter never use as substitutes for *helicopter*, even in headlines

Christ Church, Oxford (never Christ Church College). See **Peterhouse, Oxford University**

Christchurch, Dorset and New Zealand

christened people are *christened*, ships and trains etc are *named*

Christian, Christianity note also *unchristian, non-Christian, antichristian, Antichrist*

Christian Democrat noun and adjective, as in *Christian Democrat MP*

Christian names in context of non-Christians use *forename* or *first name*

Christian terms cap the Bible, the Commandments, the Cross, the Crucifixion, the Resurrection, the Gospels, Mass, Holy Communion (and simply Communion), Eucharist, Blessed Sacrament, Advent, Nativity (but note l/c when used adjectivally, eg, *a nativity play*); also use *He* and *His* when referring to God and Jesus Christ. Use l/c for *evensong, matins*. See **Churches** special section (page 172)

Christie's note apostrophe also for Christie's, New York, and Christie's International

Christmas Day, Christmas Eve

Church cap in context of the institution (Anglican, Roman Catholic, Orthodox etc), but not when used adjectivally. See **archbishops, Churches** special section (page 172)

churchwarden one word

cider (not cyder)

CIMA the Chartered Institute of Management Accountants; note caps for the abbreviation

Cincinnati, Ohio

cinemagoer similarly *concertgoer, theatregoer* etc

CinemaScope trade name, so cap; note also cap *S* in middle

cipher (not cypher)

cissy, cissies (not sissy)

Cites (not CITES); the Convention on International Trade in Endangered Species

Citizens Advice Bureau/Bureaux no apostrophe, and note final *x* as plural

Citizen's Charter

Citroën

City of London note also *the City, City prices*. See **London**

City and Guilds of London Institute abbreviate to *City & Guilds*, with ampersand

Civil List caps

Civil Service but note *civil servants*. Always cap *Civil Service*, even in adjectival use, eg, *a Civil Service memorandum*. Caps to be restored to the administrative grade, ie, *Permanent Secretary, Deputy Secretary* and *Assistant Secretary*. For executive grade (ie, below Assistant Secretary), use l/c. Note also *Secretary of the Cabinet and Head of the Home Civil Service*. See **Politics** special section (page 181)

claim do not use when simply *said* or *declared* would do. The word carries a suspicion of incredulity. Also, avoid the loose construction in sentences such as "The firm launched a drink which is claimed to promote learning ability". This should read "... a drink which, it is claimed, promotes learning ability"

clamour, clamouring but note *clamorous*

clampdown not banned, but use as little as possible

Claridge's

Clause Four (as in Labour Party policy); but Clause 4 permissible in headlines

clichés some of the most common, to be resisted strongly in almost every context, are: *backlash, basically, beleaguered, blueprint, bombshell, bonanza, brainchild, chaos, charisma, clampdown, consensus, crackdown, crisis, crunch, drama/dramatic, escalate, facelift, gunned down, hopefully, ironically, legendary, major, massive, mega-, nightmare, prestigious, quantum leap, reportedly, shambles, shock, shoot-out, situation, trauma/traumatic, unique*

C

Clinton use simply President Clinton (not President Bill Clinton), thereafter the President or Mr Clinton. The First Lady is Hillary Rodham Clinton (usually write Hillary Clinton or Mrs Clinton)

closed-circuit television

clothing use *menswear, women's wear, children's wear, sportswear*. See **wear**

cloud-cuckoo-land note two hyphens

clubs see **London clubs**

co- the prefix does not normally require a hyphen even before an *e* or another *o* unless confusion might result. Thus *co-operate* (but *uncooperative*), *co-opt, co-ordinate* (but *uncoordinated*), *coeducation, coexist*. See **co-production**

coalface, coalfield, coalmine one word; prefer *miner* to *coalminer*. Note also *gasfield, oilfield*

coastguard l/c and one word, in the British context; but note the new *Coastguard Agency* (caps), though the *coastguard service* (generic) retains the l/c. Note also the *US Coast Guard*

coasts cap *South Coast, East Coast* and *West Coast* in British context (as in *West Coast main line*); note also *East Coast* and *West Coast* in US

coats of arms see **heraldry**

Coca-Cola note hyphen; similarly *Pepsi-Cola*

Cockney cap for the person and the dialect, but l/c for general adjectival use, eg, *a cockney welcome*

coeducation(al) but *co-ed* is acceptable in headlines

coexist

Coldstream Guards may be called *the Coldstream* and the men *Coldstreamers* or *Coldstream Guards*; neither should be called *Coldstreams*. See **Armed Forces** special section (page 164)

Cold War

collarbone one word

collectibles (not -ables)

collective nouns usually use the singular verb, as with corporate bodies (the company, the Government, the council etc). But this rule is not inviolable; the key is to stick to the singular or plural throughout the story – sentences such as "The committee, which was elected recently, presented their report" are unacceptable

Colombia (country); Columbia is the Hollywood studio, university, river and Washington district. Note also British Columbia and Pre-Columbian

Colosseum, Rome but the Coliseum, London

Coloureds (South Africa); use cap

comedienne avoid wherever possible; use *comedian* for both sexes. See **feminine designations**

comeuppance no hyphen

Commander-in-Chief, Officer Commanding use caps

Commandments cap in biblical context, as *the Ten Commandments, the Fourth Commandment.* See **Christian terms**

commando note plural *commandos* (not -oes)

Commission, Commissioner see **European Commission**

Commissioner of the Metropolitan Police similarly, cap *City of London Police, British Transport Police* and all police forces when the full title is given. For full list, see **police forces**

committee note cap in *1922 Committee of Tory backbenchers.* Committees of inquiry etc should be capped only when the full title is given, eg, *the Neill Committee on Standards in Public Life,* but *the Neill committee.* Cabinet committees should be capped. See **Cabinet, select committees, royal commissions, Conservative, Tory,** and **Politics** special section (page 181)

common agricultural policy l/c; see **CAP**

Common Market usually use EU or EC (see **European Union**); but Common Market is acceptable in historical context

common sense noun; but note adjective *commonsense, commonsensical*

Common Serjeant see **Courts** special section (page 176)

Commonwealth Heads of Government Meeting use caps

communiqué

communism, communist as with *socialism* and *socialist,* the best rule is to cap only when in specific party context, eg, *a Communist candidate, a Communist rally, the Communist Mayor of Lille*; but *communist ideology, communist countries* etc. It will help to think of a parallel with Conservative/conservatism or Liberal/liberalism. But *Marxist, Stalinist, Nazi* and *Fascist* should be capped

companies abbreviate to *Co* in, eg, John Brown & Co. Company is singular. Do not confuse *company* and *firm,* even in headlines. A *firm* implies a business partnership, as in the legal or accountancy professions, estate agents etc. Full points in company titles usually unnecessary, as in WH Smith and J Sainsbury. Do not abbreviate Ford of Europe to Fords, Swan Hunter to Swans etc. See **Ltd, plc**

comparatively, relatively avoid using as synonyms of *fairly, middling*

compare with/to use *compare with* (the most common) when differences or contrasts are the point, eg, *compare the saints with the devils* or *compared with last year's figures*; use *compare to* for likenesses, eg, *compare this image to a damsel fair*

compass points in the UK, regional phrases, if well established and in common use, take caps as in the North, the South, the West, the South East, the North East, the South West, the West Country, the West Midlands, the East Midlands, East Anglia, North Wales, South Wales, West Wales, the East/West End of London. But when used adjectivally, use *southeast* England (though note the South East of England).

Overseas, cap the following: the Midwest (US), Central America, West Africa, North Africa, East Africa, Central Africa, South Africa but southern Africa, North and South Atlantic and Pacific, the Middle/Far East, but sub-Saharan Africa and south India etc

complement (completing something); but *compliment* (praise or tribute). Note also *complimentary,* as in free gifts etc

comprise means *to consist of, be composed of*; see **include**

Comptroller General

concertgoer similarly *partygoer, theatregoer,* but *concert hall*

confectionery (not -ary)

conference keep l/c in *Labour Party conference; Lib Dem conference* etc

Congo take care to distinguish between the Democratic Republic of Congo (formerly Zaire) and Congo-Brazzaville (formerly French Congo). See **Zaire**

Congress (US); note l/c *congressional* and *congressman* except when with a name, eg, Congressman John Waldorfburger; but generally try to avoid this construction and use John W, a congressman from Minnesota, etc. See **Senate**

Congress Party (India); now takes cap *P* and is no longer known as Congress (I)

connection

Connolly, Billy (comedian)

consensus (never concensus); avoid this cliché wherever possible

Conservative Party note *Conservative Central Office*, but *Conservative chairman, manifesto* etc; *Tory* is permissible as a less formal alternative, but note *Tory party* (l/c *p*). Abbreviate in lists etc to C (not Con). See **Tory, Politics** special section (page 181)

considerable avoid its use as a lazy adjective implying emphasis

Consolidated Fund, the

consortium plural *consortiums* (not consortia); as a general rule, use the *-ums* plural. Similarly *memorandums*

constitution (of a country); cap only when an actual document, eg, *the American Constitution*, but *the British constitution*

consult (never *consult with*)

Consumers' Association

Contact Group UN group on former Yugoslavia: US, Russia, Britain, France, Germany and Italy

Continent, the refers to mainland Europe; note l/c *continental*

continuous means *without intermission*; *continual* means *frequently recurring*

contract out no hyphen

Contract with America (the Republicans' 1995 programme); note italics

Contras, the cap in Nicaragua context

Controller of Radio 1 etc note cap C. See **BBC**

controversial avoid where possible

convener (not convenor)

convertible (not -able); noun and adjective

conveyor belt; a *conveyer* is a person who conveys

Cooke, Alistair (not Alastair)

cooling towers these should not be used to illustrate air pollution stories, as they emit harmless water vapour

Co-op, the acceptable abbreviation of *Co-operative Society*

co-operate, co-ordinate etc but note *uncooperative, uncoordinated, non-cooperation*

co-production, co-producer etc use hyphen to avoid ambiguity with *copro-*, as in dung

copycat (no hyphen)

copyright (sole right in artistic work etc); note *copywriter* (advertising)

cornflake (generic), but note *Kellogg's Corn Flakes*

Coronation cap *Coronation Oath* and when referring to a specific event, such as Elizabeth II's Coronation in 1953; but l/c in most adjectival uses, eg, *coronation ceremony, coronation broadcast*

coroner's court at inquests, the *coroner* is l/c unless specific, as in the Westminster Coroner. Juries *return* the verdict, the coroner *records* it. There are no coroner's inquests in Scotland; violent deaths are reported to the *Procurator Fiscal*, who may hold an inquiry. See **Courts** special section (page 176)

correspondents wherever possible, write the political correspondent of *The Times*, the Moscow correspondent of *The Times* etc; but the *Times* political correspondent, the *Times* Moscow correspondent etc, is permissible. See *The Times*

coruscating (not corruscating)

Côte d'Azur note no final *e*

councils cap in full title, eg, Birmingham City Council, otherwise l/c

council tax replacement for *poll tax/community charge*, so use the latter only in historical context

counter-productive, counter-attack etc, but *countertenor* (one word)

counties spell out names except in lists. Do not add *-shire* to Devon (except in Devonshire cream or the Duke of Devonshire), Dorset, Somerset. Irish counties should be as Co Donegal (cap C, no full point); Co Durham takes the same style. Take great care with new, reorganised or abolished counties. See **Durham, unitary authorities**

Courchevel (Alpine ski resort; not Courcheval)

court martial note plural *court s martial*; also *Courts-Martial Appeal Court*; and verb *to court-martial*

Court of Appeal always use the full title at first mention and wherever possible thereafter, though l/c *appeal court* may be used sparingly. See **Courts** special section (page 176)

Court of Arches (court of appeal of the Province of Canterbury in the Church of England); do not use *Arches Court*

Court of St James's

Court of Session, Edinburgh (not Sessions)

Court Service, the (not Courts); note caps

courts cap all courts when specific, eg, Birmingham Crown Court, Clerkenwell County Court, Dawlish Magistrates' Court, Ashford Youth Court etc; in a general, unspecific context, always cap the *Crown Court* (it sits in about 90 centres), but l/c *county court*, *magistrates' court* and *youth court* etc. See **coroner's court, Inns of Court, Courts** special section (page 176)

Coutts Bank

Coward, Noël note the diaeresis

crackdown not banned, but use as little as possible

Cracow (not Krakow or variations); see **foreign places**

crèche (not crêche)

creditworthy, creditworthiness no hyphen

Creole person born in the West Indies or Latin America whose ancestry is wholly or partly European. It does not imply mixed race

crescendo means getting louder, growing in force. Nothing *rises to a crescendo*. Plural is *crescendos*

Creutzfeldt-Jakob disease abbreviation CJD

crisis always try to find an alternative for this greatly overworked word

criterion plural *criteria*

Croat (people and language); *Croatian* is the adjective; see **Slovak**

Cross, the note cap; see **Christian terms**

cross benches but note *crossbenchers*, and adjective *crossbench*

cross-Channel but note *transatlantic*

Crown (in constitutional sense); cap, as in *Crown property, the Crown representative*. See **Royal Family**

Crown Estate Commissioners (not Estates)

Crown Jewels note caps

Crown Prosecution Service abbreviate to CPS

Crufts Show or just Crufts; note no apostrophe

cruise missiles but *Pershing missiles* and the *Stealth bomber*

crunch avoid clichés such as *reaches crunch point, the situation came to a crunch*

CSCE no longer exists; see **OSCE**

Cup cap *Final* only in *FA Cup Final* (or *Cup Final* for short), but l/c all others, such as *European Cup final, World Cup final, Davis Cup final* etc. See **Sports** special section (page 185)

cupfuls, spoonfuls etc (not cupsful or cupfulls)

currencies always convert to sterling on news, sport and features pages – usually at first mention of the foreign currency. But on Business pages, US dollars, French francs and German marks need not be converted, unless to help the flow of the story. See **deutschemark, dollar, franc** and **peseta**

current avoid wherever possible as synonym of *present*

curriculums plural *s* (not curricula); note *extracurricular activities*; abbreviate *curriculum vitae* to CV, note plural *curricula vitae*. See **national curriculum**

curtsy (not curtsey); note plural *curtsies*

Custom House (the headquarters building)

Customs and Excise cap for the organisation (or simply *Customs*), l/c for *customs officer, customs post, customs regulations* etc

cutthroat no hyphen

Cyprus, northern keep l/c in *northern*, as the "state" is recognised only by the Turkish Government; also l/c *government* in northern Cyprus, as with provincial or state governments in Australia or Canada etc

czar although usual style (in Russian context) is *tsar, czar* is permissible in the phrase *drugs czar*

Czech Republic use Czechoslovakia only in the historical sense. The two countries since their division are the Czech Republic and Slovakia

D...

dad, mum cap when referring to specific parents, l/c in general context

Dail Eireann (lower house of the Irish parliament); usually just *the Dail*

Dagestan (not Daghestan)

Dales, the Yorkshire or Derbyshire or simply *the Dales*

dancefloor

Dar es Salaam, Tanzania (no hyphens). Note, capital is Dodoma

Dark Ages caps, but take care: the period after the fall of the Roman Empire is no longer considered wholly obscure and barbaric

data strictly plural, but can be singular through common usage

databank, database

dates Note *Monday, April 18, 1994* (never 18th April); but *April 1994*. When citing periods of years, write *1992–93* (not *1992–3*) and for the millennium, *1999–2000*, then *2003–09* etc; *from 1939 to 1941* (not from *1939–41*); *the Forties, Eighties, Nineties* (or *1940s, 1980s, 1990s*). But note l/c for people's ages, eg, *she was in her forties, eighties, nineties* etc. Common usage says that the past decade ended on December 31, 1989, and that the century ends on December 31, 1999. See **millennium**

Day-Glo proprietary term, so cap

daytime but note *night-time*

daytrip but note *day-tripper*

D-Day, VE-Day, VJ-Day

deathbed no hyphen

death row (as in American prisons); l/c

debacle accents unnecessary

debatable

Debrett or full title, *Debrett's Peerage*

debut no accent

decades use either *the Sixties* or *the 1960s*; see **dates**

decimals do not mix decimals and fractions in the same story. See **millions, per cent**

decimate means to kill one in ten; custom has extended its use to indicate heavy casualties, but use sparingly

deckchair no hyphens; similarly *armchair*

decor no accent

defuse means to remove the fuse from, or reduce tension in a crisis etc; never confuse with *diffuse*, which means to spread in all directions, scatter etc, or (as adjective) verbose, not concise, spread over a large area etc

decorations see **honours**

Degas no accent

de Gaulle never cap *de* in this name unless at the start of a sentence or headline

de Havilland

de Klerk, F.W. see **full points**

de la Mare, Walter

De La Rue

DeLorean

De Niro, Robert

de Sancha, Antonia

de Valera, Eamon

degrees (educational) *a first, a second, an upper second (a 2:1), a lower second (a 2:2), a third* etc. D Lit, D Litt, LitD etc are abbreviations for doctorates of literature (or letters); Oxford and York have D Phil instead of the more usual PhD. Oxford has DM for the more usual MD. Cambridge has ScD for doctor of science. No full points in degrees

degrees (weather) omit degree sign in temperatures. See **celsius**

déjà vu use accents but not italic

demise strictly means the death of a person, or the failure of an enterprise or institution. Keep to these definitions. It is wrong to refer to the demise of Glenn Hoddle or Peter Mandelson

Democratic Party (US; not Democrat Party); the adjective is usually *Democrat* in other uses, such as *the Democrat spokesman* (but note *the Democratic convention*)

demonstrator but note *protester*

Deng, Wendi Rupert Murdoch's wife; see **Murdoch**

Denktas, Rauf (not Denktash), the president of northern Cyprus (l/c *p* because not an internationally recognised state); better to describe him as the *Turkish Cypriot leader*. See **Cyprus**

deny does not mean the same as *rebut* (which means argue to the contrary, producing evidence), or *refute* (which means to win such an argument). See **rebut, refute**

Department for Culture, Media and Sport (not of) replaced the Department of National Heritage in July 1997. *Culture Secretary* is an acceptable short form for the Secretary of State

Department for Education and Employment (not of); use *Education and Employment Department* or *the department* at subsequent mentions. Avoid the ugly abbreviations DfE or DfEE except in direct quotes

Department of the Environment, Transport and the Regions

dependant noun; note *dependent* (adj), and *dependency*

Deputy Prime Minister caps; similarly *Deputy Governor of the Bank of England*. Note these are the exceptions to the rule that deputy posts should take l/c, eg, *deputy editor*

desiccate

desktop (computer, publishing), no hyphen; similarly *laptop*

despite acceptable alternative for *in spite of*. But do not use *despite the fact that*; use *although* instead

despoiled (not despoilt)

despoliation, or **despoilment** (not despoilation)

deutschemark/deutschmark/D-mark never use these forms. Always use simply *the mark*, or with figures, *DM500*. See **currencies**

Deutsche Bank German commercial bank not to be confused with *Deutsche Bundesbank*, or *Bundesbank*, the German central bank

D

Devil, the cap; but note *devils* (l/c), *devilish*

dextrous prefer to dexterous

Dhaka (capital of Bangladesh; not Dacca)

Diaghilev

diagnose take great care: *illnesses* are diagnosed, not patients

Diana, Princess of Wales since her death, use the form *the late Princess* where appropriate. Never use Princess Di or Lady Di. Note also one comma only for *the Diana, Princess of Wales Memorial Fund.* See **Royal Family, Titles** special section (page 187)

Diaspora cap in Jewish context, but l/c in general sense of a dispersal

Di Canio, Paulo (cap Di every time)

DiCaprio, Leonardo

Dickins & Jones (department store)

Dictaphone trade name, so cap

diehard

different from (never different to or than*); similarly *differ from*

dignitaries

dilapidated (not delapidated)

dilate *dilation* means normal widening, as in pupils of the eye; *dilatation* is widening by force, as in child abuse cases. Take care

Dillons (bookshop)

dining room (no hyphen)

diphtheria note *ph*; similarly *diphthong*

Diplomatic Service caps; similarly *Civil Service*

directives (EU); l/c in general context, caps when specific, eg, *Working Time Directive*

Direct Line, Direct Line Insurance trademarks, so must not be used in generic sense even with l/c, as in direct line companies, direct line telephone insurers etc; in this wider sense, use *direct insurance, direct telephone insurance* etc

Director of Public Prosecutions abbreviation DPP

Director-General of the BBC, CBI, Institute of Directors, Fair Trading, and the regulatory bodies etc. See **regulators, Secretary-General**

Directory Enquiries (despite usual style, *inquiries*)

disc (musical recording, or shape, eg, *disc jockey, compact disc, disc brake*); but use *disk* in general computing context, eg, *disk drive, floppy disk*

discomfit take great care with this verb; it means primarily to thwart, defeat or rout, but by extension can mean thoroughly to embarrass or disconcert (noun *discomfiture*). It has no connection with discomfort, which means to deprive of comfort or make uneasy

discreet means tactful, circumspect (noun *discretion*); *discrete* means individually distinct (noun *discreteness*)

disinterested means impartial, unbiased (noun *disinterest*); never confuse with *uninterested*, which means having a lack of interest

Disney the theme parks are *Disneyland* (California); *Disney World* (Florida); *Disneyland Paris* (Euro Disney should strictly be confined to the name of the European company); and *Tokyo Disneyland* (owned by a Japanese company, but Disney earns royalties from it)

disorientate (not disorient). See **orientate**

dispatch (not despatch); also *dispatch box*

dissociate (not disassociate)

distil but note *distilled, distillation*

divorcé (man); note *divorcée* (woman), use *divorcees* (no accent) in reference to both men and women

DIY spell out *do-it-yourself* at first mention

D-notice, D-notice committee

Docklands note cap *D* for London, elsewhere *docklands*

doctor the title *Dr* should no longer be confined to medical practitioners. If a person has a doctorate from a reputable institution, and wishes to be known as Dr Smith, he or she should be so titled

docusoap, docudrama etc (no hyphens)

dogs l/c with most breeds, such as *alsatian, borzoi, labrador, rottweiler*, though there are obvious exceptions such as West Highland terrier, Yorkshire terrier etc

Dole, Bob (not Robert)

dollar with figures use $5 (when American), A$5 (Australian), C$5 (Canadian), S$5 (Singapore)

doll's house (not dolls')

Dome cap *D* in *Millennium Dome* and when used on its own. See **millennium**

Domesday Book roman, similarly Magna Carta; but note *doomsday* in general or biblical sense

Dominican Republic (neighbour to Haiti); note *Dominica*, one of the Windward Islands. Both are sovereign states. See **Haiti**

donate use *give* or *present* wherever possible

Dorchester, the (not Dorchester Hotel)

do's and don'ts

Dostoevsky

doveish (rather than dovish)

down avoid unnecessary use after verbs, as in close down, shut down. See **up**

Downing Street write *10 Downing Street* (or *11. . .*), or simply *No 10*; note *Downing Street policy unit*. See **Politics** special section (page 181)

Downing Street declaration see **Ireland**

downmarket no hyphen; similarly *upmarket*

Down's syndrome (never mongol)

Down Under cap as a colloquialism for Australasia (especially Australia)

D'Oyly Carte

D-Rams note also *CD-Roms*

drachmas (not drachmae)

draconian note l/c

draftsman (legal); but note *draughtsman* (art, design)

drama, dramatic confine their use to the theatrical context wherever possible; *dramatic events* and the like are overworked clichés

Dr Dolittle (italics for the film, roman for the character)

dreamt (not dreamed)

drier (comparative of dry); note *dryer* (noun), as in *tumble dryer*

drink-drive, drink-driver, drink-driving note that the limits are 35 *micrograms* of alcohol per 100 millilitres of *breath*; and 80 *milligrams* of alcohol per 100 millilitres of *blood*

drivers no hyphens in *taxi driver*, *bus driver*, *car driver* etc

drop a bombshell avoid this cliché

dropout noun or adjective as in students; note *drop-out* (rugby); and *to drop out* (verb)

drugs do not confuse *narcotics* (which include cocaine and heroin) with other illicit drugs such as cannabis, LSD and amphetamines

Drug Enforcement Administration (US); thereafter DEA

Druid(s) cap

Druze (religious sect and militia group in Lebanon)

Dr Who roman for the character (subsequent mentions *the Doctor*), but italics for the programme

dry-clean, dry-cleaning etc

drystone wall

dual of two, eg, *dual carriageway*; note *duel* (fight)

du Cann, (Sir) Edward

Duchess of York no longer a member of the Royal Family since her divorce. After first mention as Duchess of York, refer to *the duchess* (l/c) subsequently – never Fergie or any such vulgarity. See **Titles** special section (page 187)

due to must not be used as the equivalent of *because of* or *owing to*. The phrase must be attached to a noun or pronoun: "His absence was due to illness" is correct; "He was absent due to illness" is wrong

duffel bag, duffel coat

Duke of Edinburgh write the Duke (cap) or Prince Philip after first mention; but this cap rule applies only to the British Royal Family and overseas heads of state, so the Duke of Rutland would become *the duke* (l/c) after first mention. See **Royal Family, heads of state, Titles** special section (page 189)

dump do not use as synonym of *dismiss* or *sack*

Durham use Co Durham for the county and (if any question of ambiguity) Durham city for the city; see **counties**

duty-free hyphenate noun and adjective

dwarf as plural, prefer *dwarfs* (not dwarves); avoid "politically correct" circumlocutions such as *person of restricted growth*

dyke (embankment; not dike)

dysentery (not dysentry or disentery)

dyspepsia

E...

each, every although singular, they are acceptable now with plural pronouns, as the plural is increasingly a way of avoiding "he or she", or "his or her". Hence, "everyone has what they want", "each of us has our secrets", but "everyone has secrets"

Earhart, Amelia (1930s aviatrix)

Earls Court no apostrophe

early hours avoid the phrase *in the early hours of the morning*; write simply *the early hours* or, better, *early yesterday/today*

earned (never earnt)

earring no hyphen

Earth cap only in planetary or astronomical sense, not in phrases such as *down to earth*. The same rule applies to Moon and Sun. See **Universe**

earthquake can abbreviate to *quake* in headings. See **Richter scale**

east, eastern for when to cap, see **compass points**

East End also West End of London; and East, West, North, South, Central, Inner London. See **London**

EastEnders (TV soap opera)

Easter Day (not Easter Sunday)

Eastern Europe but note *eastern Germany*. See **Germany**

easygoing

easyJet

EBRD European Bank for Reconstruction and Development

EC must not be used as an abbreviation for the European Commission in text or headlines. EC remains the short form only of the European Community, although in almost all contexts now, EU is preferred. See **European Commission, European Union**

E.coli italics in text, but roman and no point in headlines

e-commerce (as *e-mail*)

ecosystem no hyphen, but note *eco-warrior*

Ecstasy (drug)

ecu (European currency unit)

Ecuadorean (not -ian)

ecumenical (not oecumenical, but respect titles). See **Churches** special section (page 172)

editor cap first mention of editors of well-known leading publications, such as the Editor of *The Times,* Editor of *The Mirror,* Editor of the *Yorkshire Post,* Editor of *The Spectator;* subsequent mentions, revert to l/c. Similarly, Editor-in-Chief. Note that deputy editors and below retain l/c. See **job titles, newspapers**

education action zones (EAZs), l/c in general context but cap specifics, eg, Barnsley Education Action Zone. Similar style to *local education authorities* (LEAs)

educationist (not educationalist)

eg no points, but use a comma before and after. See **ie**

Eire do not use except in historical context. See **Ireland**

eisteddfod l/c except when naming a particular one in full, eg, the International Eisteddfod at Llangollen; note plural *eisteddfodau*

either takes a singular verb when both subjects are embraced, eg, *either is good enough.* See **neither**

elderly, aged, old be sensitive in the use of these words, and generally do not use for people under 65

electrocardiographs (machines for measuring heart function); note *electrocardiograms,* the tracings made by electrocardiographs

electrocute means to kill by electric shock

Elgin Marbles subsequently the *Marbles*

elicit means to evoke, bring to light, or draw out; never confuse with *illicit* (unlawful, forbidden)

elite roman, no accent

e-mail

embarkation (not embarcation). You *embark in* (not on) a ship. See **Armed Forces** special section (page 164)

embarrass(ment) but note the French *embarras de choix, embarras de richesses*

Embassy same style as for *Ambassador*, eg, *the French Embassy in Rome*, thereafter *the embassy*

Emmies plural of the *Emmy awards*

emphasise prefer this to *stress* in phrases such as "he emphasised the importance", "she emphasised that the ruling was final". See **stress**

empire cap as in *British* or *Roman Empire*; similarly, cap *emperor* when specific, eg, Emperor Claudius

employment tribunals have replaced industrial tribunals. See **industrial tribunals**

EMS European Monetary System

EMU economic and monetary union (in Europe); see **ERM**

encyclopaedia (not encyclopedia)

England, English beware of these when the meaning is *Britain, British*

England and Wales Cricket Board has replaced the TCCB, and is abbreviated as ECB; do not shorten to England/English Cricket Board. See **Sports** special section (page 185)

enormity does not mean great size; it means quality or character of being outrageous, or extreme wickedness or serious error. Do not misuse. For great size, use *immensity*

en route not italics

ensign the *White Ensign* is the ensign of the Royal Navy and the Royal Yacht Squadron; the *Red Ensign* is the British Merchant Navy's flag; the *Blue Ensign* is flown by Royal Fleet Auxiliary vessels and by certain yacht clubs. There is no such thing as the Royal Ensign; however, the *Royal Standard* will fly from one of the Queen's homes when she is there. See **Royal Standard**

ensure means to make certain; you *insure* against risk; you *assure* your life. The verb *ensure* usually needs *that* after it if accompanied by a following verb (eg, "he tried to ensure that the policy was adopted"); but omit *that* if followed by a noun (eg, "he tried to ensure its success")

enthral

Environment Agency note caps

Equator cap, but *equatorial* in general sense

ERM exchange-rate mechanism (in European contexts); a part of the wider concept of EMU

escalate, escalation avoid these clichés; use *rise, grow* or *soar* instead

escapers (never escapees)

Eskimo plural *Eskimos*; preferred to Inuit

Establishment, the cap in sense of the perceived leaders of society; but l/c as in the *medical establishment*, the *legal establishment*, when the sense is more restricted

Eucharist cap; see **Christian terms**

euro (European common currency); note l/c (as franc, pound, mark, peseta etc); also *eurozone* or *euroland* for the single currency area

eurocheques, eurobonds l/c, no hyphen

Europe note caps for Western, Eastern, Central. Europe includes the British Isles, so do not use the name as equivalent to the Continent. Britain does not export to Europe, but to the *rest* of Europe

European Commission, Commissioners cap *Commission* throughout as a noun, but l/c when adjectival, eg, a *commission ruling* (the same rule as for Government/government); cap *commissioner* only when referring to a specific person (eg, Mario Monti, the Competition Commissioner; thereafter, *the commissioner*). The President of the European Commission is capped throughout (as with all foreign Presidents)

European Economic Area (EEA) European tariff-free zone, comprising the 15 members of the EU plus Norway, Iceland and Liechtenstein

European Parliament Members of the European Parliament (MEPs), or Euro MPs

European Union (EU), European Community (EC) the first is now the preferred phrase except where the context is trade. If you must use *the*

Union, cap it throughout, but wherever possible use EU. Use *Common Market* and *EEC* only in historical context

Eurosceptic no longer hyphenated; similarly *Europhobia, Europhiles*

Eurotunnel one word; note that *Le Shuttle* no longer exists – the shuttle trains are now also called Eurotunnel trains. *Eurostar* passenger trains continue as before; see **Channel Tunnel**

evensong l/c; see **matins, Christian terms**

eventuate avoid; use *happen* instead

ever rarely necessary; avoid phrases such as *best-ever, fastest-ever*, and use simply *best* and *fastest,* qualifying (where appropriate) with *yet.* See **first, superlatives, universal claims**

ex- prefer *former* in most contexts, as in *former Yugoslavia,* though *ex-serviceman* is unavoidable and *ex-* is fine for headlines

examinations *11-plus, 7-plus* etc; also *A levels,* but *A-level results* etc (hyphenate only when adjectival). Abbreviate to *exam* only in headlines. GCSE, the General Certificate of Secondary Education, need not normally be spelt out

excepting do not use when *except* or *except for* is possible

exclamation marks nearly always unnecessary

exclusive avoid with story or interview. The phrase "in an interview with *The Times*" is sufficient

execution take care: as with *assassination,* do not use as a synonym of any killing or murder. An execution is a judicial killing after due process of law

exhibitions titles of art exhibitions now in italics. See **Arts** special section (page 169)

existing use *present* wherever possible as an alternative

Exocet note cap

expatriate (not ex-patriate and never expatriot); noun, verb or adjective

Export Credits Guarantee Department abbreviate to ECGD; note *Credits* plural

extramarital no hyphen; similarly *extramural, extracurricular, extrasensory* etc

exuberant (never exhuberant); but note *exhilarate, exhort*

eye of a storm do not refer to the *calm in the eye of the storm*; the eye, by definition, is the calm area at the centre of a storm or hurricane

eye to eye no hyphens

eyeing

eyewitness use *witness* instead wherever possible (except in direct quotes)

F...

F111s no hyphen; see **aircraft types**

façade use the cedilla

facelift use sparingly in its metaphorical sense, where it has become overworked. In cosmetic context quite acceptable, however

fact that almost always an unnecessary circumlocution, so avoid, eg, "owing to the fact that" means *because*

fact sheet

Faeroe Isles or *the Faeroes*

fahrenheit see **celsius**

fairytale no hyphen

Faithfull, Marianne

falangist (Spain); note *phalangist* (Lebanon)

fallacy means a *faulty argument*, not an erroneous belief

fallout noun; no longer hyphenated

fan acceptable nowadays for football supporter or pop music enthusiast

Far East encompasses the following: China, Hong Kong, Japan, North and South Korea, Macau, Mongolia, Taiwan. See **Asean, South-East Asia**

farther is applied only to distance (literal or figurative), eg, "nothing could be farther from the truth". *Further* means *in addition to,* *another,* eg, "a further point"

fascia (not facia)

Fascist cap in the political sense, but as a term of abuse, l/c; but note *fascism* l/c except in specifically party context. See **communism**

Father (as in priest); avoid the ugly abbreviation Fr before a name

Father's Day (not Fathers'). See **Mother's Day**

fatwa (Muslim religious edict, not a sentence of punishment); not italic

fault-line (hyphenate)

Fayed, Dodi (the late elder son of Mohamed Al Fayed; not Dodi Al Fayed)

Fed, the (US); use *Federal Reserve* (Board not usually necessary) at first mention; cap the *Chairman* of the Fed, as with *Governor of the Bank of England, President of the Bundesbank* etc

Federal Aviation Administration (US); abbreviation FAA; (not Agency or Authority)

"feel-good" factor

Fellow cap in specific title such as Dr Arthur Brown, a Fellow of Magdalen, or in the more obvious Fellow of the Royal College of Surgeons (FRCS); but l/c in general sense, eg, *a group of fellows in the quadrangle*; keep *fellowship* l/c

female do not write, for example, *female councillors, female directors;* instead use (where gender is relevant) *women councillors, women directors* etc

feminine designations *authoress, poetess, wardress* etc should be avoided. But *actress* is such common usage that it is acceptable. See **comedienne**

Ferris wheel

Festival Hall generally omit *Royal*

festivals cap the Edinburgh Festival (cultural), Reading Festival (pop), Cheltenham Festival (racing) etc, thereafter *the festival* (l/c). See **Fringe**

fête with accent

fewer of numbers, eg, *fewer people, fewer goals;* use *less with* size, quantity, or singular nouns, eg, *less population, less meat.* See **less**

fiancé (man), note **fiancée** (woman); see **divorcé**

Fianna Fail, Fine Gael see **Ireland**

Fide (world chess body; not FIDE); see **chess names**

fifty write *50-50 chance*; note cap for the decade, eg, *Fifties*, but l/c for age, eg, *she was in her fifties*

fighting for his/her life avoid this meaningless phrase. Instead use *critically ill/injured*

figures see **numbers**

filibuster (not fillibuster)

Filipinos, Filipinas (women), **the Philippines** (country)

films titles in italics; see **Arts** special section (page 169); note *film-maker*; see **movies**

film star two words

Financial Services Authority (FSA) has replaced the Securities and Investments Board (SIB)

fiord (not fjord)

firearms do not confuse bullets with shotgun cartridges (containing pellets); a gunshot wound is markedly different from a bullet wound

fire brigade l/c in general context, but cap specifics, eg, *Kent Fire Brigade*

firefight should not be used as a synonym of *military skirmish* or *exchange of fire*; *firefighters* try to extinguish flames

firm do not use as a synonym of *company*. See **companies**

first serves as an adverb, so avoid *firstly*. If a list of priorities is essential in a story, write *first, secondly, thirdly* etc. Never use *first-ever*. See **ever, superlatives, universal claims**

first aid noun, no hyphen; but hyphenate when adjectival, eg, *first-aid qualifications*

First World War (not World War One); similarly *Second World War*. See **wars**

Fitzgerald, Garret

Five Nations Championship (initial caps) becomes the *Six Nations Championship* in 2000 (England, Wales, Scotland, Ireland, France and Italy)

flair (as in talent); do not confuse with *flare* (as in fire, fashion etc)

flat-owners hyphen, but note *homeowners*

flaunt means to make an ostentatious or defiant display, eg, *she flaunted her finery*; to *flout* is to show contempt for, eg, *he flouted the law*

fledgeling

fleur-de-lys (not lis)

flight numbers cap in stories where the number of the flight is relevant, eg, *Flight 103* (Lockerbie disaster)

floodlighting but note *floodlit*

flotation (shares), but note *floatation* (tanks)

flout see **flaunt**

flowerbed one word; similarly *flowerpot*

flu no apostrophe; acceptable abbreviation for *influenza*

Flushing Meadows (New York home of the US Open tennis championships; not Meadow)

Flying Squad cap, as it is the only one in the UK. But l/c *fraud squads* as there are several; similarly *vice squads, drug squads, crime squads, regional crime squads*

focused

folk-song, folk-singer (use hyphen)

following do not use as synonym of *after*. Always use *after* instead

Food and Drug Administration (US)

foodstuffs where place names form part of the phrase, generally use the cap, eg, *Brussels sprouts, Cheddar cheese, chicken Kiev, Cornish pasties, potatoes Lyonnaise*; but keep l/c for *hamburger, frankfurter* etc. See **metric**

foolproof no hyphen

foot-and-mouth disease

football *soccer* is now an acceptable synonym of *association football*. See **Premiership**

for-, fore- the general rule is that *e* is added only when the prefix has the meaning of *before*. Thus *forbears* (refrains), *forebears* (ancestors); *forgo* (go without), *forego* (go before, as in *foregone conclusion*). Take particular care with *forswear* and *foresee(able)*, both frequently misspelt

Forces use the *Armed Forces* wherever possible, but if the word has to be used alone, cap *Forces* both as a noun and adjectivally (as *Service*). See **Armed Forces** special section (page 164)

Foreign and Commonwealth Office usually shorten to *Foreign Office* or *FCO* (abbreviation permissible in headlines); no longer use *FO*

foreign appellations *The Times* uses local honorifics for:
France: M, Mme, Mlle and Me (for Maître, legal)
Germany and **Austria:** Herr, Frau, Fräulein
Spain and Spanish-speaking **Latin America:** Señor, Señora, Señorita
Italy: Signor, Signora, Signorina
Portugal and **Brazil:** Senhor, Senhora (but not Senhorina)
Note that with Belgium, Luxembourg, Switzerland and Canada, Mr, Mrs, Miss, Ms etc are used because of those countries' linguistic sensitivities, eg, Jacques Santer, former President of the European Commission, will subsequently be Mr Santer. Similarly the English forms with Francophone Africa, where French is more the language of the elite rather than the lingua franca.

For all other nationalities, use English except where it is possible to use a local title (eg, *Ayatollah, Begum, Chief, Pandit, Sheikh*), or a military one (eg, Colonel Gaddafi); occasionally, where titles are in general use (eg, Baron von X in Germany), we would respect such exceptions.

Note in Burma, U means Mr, Daw means Mrs; in China, the first Chinese name is the surname, eg, Deng Xiaoping becomes Mr Deng

foreign places as a general rule, use the spellings in *The Times Atlas of the World,* including Chinese place names (see **Chinese names**). However, *The Times* retains the Anglicised or commonly accepted spellings of many familiar (and especially European) countries and cities, such as *Brussels, Cologne, Cracow, Dunkirk, Florence, Geneva, Gothenburg, The Hague, Lyons, Majorca, Marseilles, Mexico City, Minorca, Moscow, Munich, Naples, Prague, Rheims, Rome, Salonika, Venice.* See also **Spanish regions**

foreign words write in roman when foreign words and phrases have become essentially a part of the English language (eg, an elite, a debacle, a fête); otherwise, use italic (eg, a *bon mot*, a *bête noire,* the *raison d'être*). Avoid pretension by using an English phrase wherever one will serve. See **accents**

forensic means *pertaining to the courts*. A forensic expert could be a solicitor or a biochemist; make your meaning clear by writing *forensic scientist, forensic medicine* etc

for ever means *always*; note *forever* means *continuously*

forklift truck

Formica proprietary term, so cap

formula plural usually *formulas*, but use *formulae* in mathematical contexts

fortuitous does not mean *fortunate*. It means *by chance* or *accidental*. Do not confuse

forum plural *forums*; see **referendum**

four-letter words avoid where possible, but if there is no alternative (eg, in direct quotes, where they are essential to the story), soften them with asterisks, eg, f***, c*** etc. See **obscenities**

foxhunt, foxhunting without hyphens, similarly *foxhound*, *foxhole*, *master of foxhounds* (l/c *m*)

fractions do not mix fractions and decimals in the same story. Compounds such as *half-hour*, *half-dozen* etc take a hyphen; *half an hour*, *half a dozen* do not. Hyphenate when fractions are adjectival, eg, *two-thirds full*, but not as nouns, eg, *two thirds of the bus was empty*. See **two thirds**

framework document (Anglo-Irish proposals for Northern Ireland, February 1995) note l/c; full title of the document is *Frameworks for the Future*. See **Ireland**

franc l/c, and abbreviate as *Fr40*; specify if not French, eg, *BFr40 (Belgian)*, *SwFr40 (Swiss)*

franchisor (no longer franchiser)

Frankenstein foods never use this pejorative phrase to describe genetically modified (GM) foods, except in direct quotations

fraud squad l/c; see **Flying Squad**

free avoid the modern cliché *for free* when the meaning is simply *free*

"freebie" just permissible as colloquialism for *handout*, *free trip* etc, but use inverted commas

Free Churches, Free Churchman caps

freefall no hyphen

Freemasonry, Mason, Masonic

French names prefer the more Anglicised style for street names etc, eg,

Rue Royale, Place de la Victoire, Boulevard des Montagnes. No need to hyphenate place names such as St Malo, St Etienne etc

french windows l/c

frescoes (not frescos)

Freud, Lucian (not Lucien)

Fringe, the Edinburgh always cap, whether as noun or adjective

Frisbee proprietary term, so cap

front bench, the noun; but note *frontbencher, frontbench power* etc. See **Politics** special section (page 181)

frontline adjective, as in the *frontline states*; but note the noun *front line*

front-runner

FTSE 100 index no longer hyphenate FT-SE; note also the *FTSE all-share index*

fuchsia

fuel greatly overworked verb, especially in headlines; always seek alternatives such as *raise, increase, add to, boost*

Fujiyama, or **Mount Fuji** (not Mount Fujiyama)

fulfil but note *fulfilled, fulfilling*

full points note thin space after initials and points, eg, F. W. de Klerk. But with companies, omit the full points, eg, WH Smith. See **companies, initials**

-ful, -fuls so *cupfuls* (not cupsful)

full-time adj, but note noun *full time* (as in football)

fulsome be very careful – and sparing – with the use of this word. It means *excessive* or *insincere* (the cliché *fulsome praise* actually means excessive praise, not generous or warm praise). Try to avoid it, especially the cliché

fundholders (NHS)

fundraising, fundraiser no hyphen

further see **farther**

fusillade

G...

Gaddafi, Colonel Muammar (Libyan leader)

gaff (hook or spar); but *gaffe* (blunder or indiscretion). Note *to blow the gaff* (let out a secret)

Gambia, The always cap the definite article

gambit (technical term in chess, meaning an opening involving a sacrifice in return for general advantage); *opening gambit* is thus tautological. Take care with its use as a metaphor, and use sparingly

game show no hyphen; similarly *chat show*, *quiz show*, *talk show* etc

Gandhi, Mahatma, Indira etc (never Ghandi)

Garda see **Ireland**

Gardeners' Question Time (not Gardener's)

gas, gases noun; but *gassed*, *gassing* (verbal use); note also *gases* (not gasses) for present tense, eg, *doctor gases patient*

gasfield similarly *coalfield, oilfield*

Gatt the General Agreement on Tariffs and Trade. Its successor body is now the *World Trade Organisation* (WTO). See **Uruguay Round, World Trade Organisation**

Gatwick sufficiently well-known not to need airport in title. See **airports, Heathrow**

gauge (not guage)

Gaultier, Jean Paul no hyphen

gay where possible, use *homosexual* or *lesbian*, but *gay* has become such common currency that we should avoid looking or sounding pompous in this context. See **straight**

GCSE see **examinations**

GDP gross domestic product

GEC Alsthom became simply *Alstom* (note no "h") in mid-1998

gelatine rather than gelatin

Geldof, Bob do not write *Sir* Bob Geldof, as he is an honorary KBE

gender (term of grammar); do not use as synonym of a person's sex

general election always l/c

General Secretary of the TUC caps; but note l/c for *general secretary* of individual unions; see **TUC**

General Strike (of 1926); caps

General Synod (of the Church of England), thereafter *the synod*. See **Churches** special section (page 172)

Gentile(s) cap

geriatric does not mean *elderly,* but is applied to medical treatment for the elderly, eg, *geriatric hospital.* Never use as a term of abuse

German Bight (as in shipping forecast; not Bite)

Germany full title is the *Federal Republic of Germany.* If referring to the area that was East Germany, say *eastern Germany* or the *former East Germany*; similarly *western Germany* or the *former West Germany.* *Ossis, Wessis* permissible vernacular for inhabitants of the two parts

gerrymander

get, got a lazy verb, so avoid where possible

Getty, Sir Paul do not use John or J. in his name any longer

Ghanaian (not Ghanian)

ghetto use only in the sense of an area of enforced or customary segregation, not as an ethnic neighbourhood, eg, middle-class *district,* not *ghetto.* Note plural *ghettos*

giant-killer, giant-killing

gibe means *taunt* or *sneer*; note also *gybe* meaning to *shift direction* or *change course,* particularly in sailing. For the sake of clarity, *jibe* (a variant of both) should no longer be used

Gibraltar (never Gibralter); note *Strait of Gibraltar* (not Straits)

gig acceptable for a musical event; similarly *rave*

gillie rather than ghillie

gipsy see **gypsy**

girl do not use as a synonym of *woman*

girlfriend one word; similarly *boyfriend.* Use *girlfriend* only for young people; otherwise *woman friend* or just *friend* (where the gender is obvious)

Girl Guides now simply *Guides*; see **Boy Scouts**

giro (l/c), as in benefit payments, cheques etc

Giscard d'Estaing, Valéry thereafter M Giscard

giveaway noun or adjective; one word, similarly *takeaway*; but note *to give away*

glamorise, glamorous but note *glamour*

glasnost not italic

glassmaker

Glen Coe (valley); but note *Glencoe* (battle, village and pass)

Glorious Twelfth, the caps

GMB write the GMB general union

gobbledegook

God cap when referring to just one, in any religion. *He, His, Him* are also capped. When non-specific, use l/c, eg, *Greek gods*. See **Christian terms, Churches** special section (page 172)

godforsaken but note *God-fearing*

godparents, godfather, godmother, godson, goddaughter, godchild

Goebbels, Joseph (not Goebells etc)

-goer as a suffix, run on as one word, as in *churchgoer, partygoer, theatregoer* etc

Goldeneye (James Bond film; not GoldenEye)

Golders Green no apostrophe

goldmine, goldmining

Goldsmiths College, London no longer use apostrophe

goodbye

goodwill one word, whether used as a noun or adjective

Gorazde, Bosnia (not Goradze)

Gorbachev, Mikhail

gorilla

Gormley, Antony (the sculptor)

Gothenburg (not Göteborg)

Gothic cap; preferable to Gothick

Government cap all governments, British and overseas, when referring to a specific one, eg, "the Government resigned last night", "the Argentine Government sent troops", and specific past administrations such as "the Heath Government"; only l/c when unspecific or one that has yet to be formed, eg, "all the governments since the war", or "the next Tory government would raise pensions".

Also l/c government in all adjectival contexts, eg, *a government minister*, *a government decision*, *government expenditure*. A further instance of l/c use is in phrases such as *the Bosnian government troops* or *the British government-backed trade delegation*, when the use is again principally adjectival.

Also, note that provincial or state governments in Australia, Canada, India etc retain l/c. See **Politics** special section (page 181)

government departments cap both when giving full title (eg, *Department of Trade and Industry*), and even when abbreviated, as in *Health Department*, *Education Department*, *Trade Department* etc. The same applies to *ministries*, home and overseas

Governor (of the Bank of England); cap at every mention, also cap Deputy Governor of the Bank. Also, cap the Governor of Hong Kong at every mention; but cap prison governors at first mention only, eg, James X, Governor of Parkhurst, thereafter l/c, and l/c deputy governors

Graces *The Three Graces* (Canova's statue). See **Arts** special section (page 169)

Grade II listed, Grade II* listed etc

gram (not gramme); similarly *kilogram*; see **metric**

grandad but note *granddaughter*

Grand Jury (caps) in US contexts

grandmaster (chess); l/c. See **chess names**

Grappelli, Stéphane

grassroots adjective; note the noun *grass roots*. Use this cliché sparingly

great and the good, the all l/c; quotes usually unnecessary

greater or lesser degree *lesser* is not correct but is common usage

Great Ormond Street Hospital for Children (no longer Sick Children)

Greco- (not Graeco-)

green belt l/c

Green Paper caps; see **White Paper**

Green Party, or **the Greens** but note *green issues* etc

grisly means *horrifying, repugnant*; note *grizzly* which means *greyish, grizzled*, or is a short form of *grizzly bear*

grottoes

ground(s) in the sense of *reason*, do not use plural unless more than one is given; eg, "he gave up his job on the ground of illness"; but "he gave up his job on the grounds of his failed marriage and illness"

Group 4 (security company)

G-string

guerrilla beware of loaded terms for advocates of political violence; see **terrorist**

guesthouse no hyphen

guidebook similarly *chequebook, stylebook, textbook, formbook* etc

Guildhall, London (never *the* Guildhall)

guinea-pig (hyphen)

Gulf, the avoid the term *Persian Gulf* as it angers Iraqis and many other Arabs

gunboat, gunfight, gunfire, gunman, gunpoint, gunshot, gunsmith but note *gun dog*

gunned down avoid this Americanism; instead say *shot dead*

gunwales (nautical, not gunwhales)

Gurkhas

guttural (not gutteral)

Guyana (formerly British Guiana, now independent); do not confuse with *French Guiana* (French overseas territory)

Gypsy/gypsy (not gipsy). Cap when referring to a specific group of this semi-nomadic people, but l/c in the more general sense of somebody constantly on the move, eg, "the Gypsies on Epsom Downs threatened to retaliate"; but "police said they would chase all gypsies from the county". The other wandering groups in Britain are the Irish tinkers, who prefer the name *Irish travellers*; the *Scottish tinkers* (or *tinklers*); and the hippies, whom we can call *New Age travellers*; *travellers* is a useful generic term

H...

Häagen-Dazs (brand of ice-cream originating in America)

Haberdashers' Aske's School, Elstree

Habsburg no longer Hapsburg

haemorrhage means heavy and potentially dangerous bleeding, not simply bleeding. Beware of misuse in metaphor

Hague, Ffion follow Cherie Blair/Booth style for William's wife: *Ffion Hague* (or *Mrs Hague*) when with her husband, but *Ffion Jenkins* (subsequently *Ms Jenkins*) when at functions in her own right

Hague, The

hairdresser, hairbrush, haircut, hairdryer, hairpin, hairstyle

Haiti, Haitian note that Haiti must never be described as an island; it is joined to the Dominican Republic and together they constitute the island of Hispaniola

haj (pilgrimage to Mecca); l/c and roman

haka (Maori war-dance); l/c and roman

half-time (in football match etc); note the *half time* in business context, but hyphenate when used adjectivally, eg, *half-time results*

halfway no hyphen; but note *half-hearted*

Halley's comet see **heavenly bodies**

Hallowe'en

handmade, handbuilt (no hyphen)

handout as a noun, no hyphen

hangar (aircraft); note *hanger* (clothes)

hanged "The murderer was hanged at dawn" – note never *hung*. Clothes are hung on a washing line or a hanger

Hansard

harass, harassment

hardcore one word as adjective, eg, *hardcore pornography*; but note two words as noun, eg, *the hard core of the rebels*; similarly *hard core* (rubble)

hardline adjective; but note *to take a hard line*

Haringey (London borough and council); note also *Harringay* (London neighbourhood)

HarperCollins, or **HarperCollins Publishers** owned by The News Corporation; see **News International**

Harpers & Queen

Harrods no apostrophe; see **Al Fayed**

harvest festival l/c

Hattersley, Lord (not "of Sparkbrook")

Havisham, Miss (not Miss Haversham) in Dickens's *Great Expectations*

Hawaiian

hay fever no hyphen

headache avoid as a synonym of *difficulty*

head-butt noun or verb

headhunt, headhunting, headhunter no hyphens

headlines avoid the worst clichés and hyperboles such as *bash*, *crash*, *shock*, *slam* etc; but words such as *bid* (for attempt), *crisis*, *hit* (adversely affect), *row* (clash or dispute) and *phone* (telephone) – all of which should not normally appear in text – are permissible in headlines, provided they are not overworked

Inverted commas must always be single in headlines, straps and display panels. See **quotation marks**

headmaster, headmistress one word and l/c except in the formal, official title (and then cap at first mention only). Some schools have variants on the usual style; Eton, Harrow, Rugby and Westminster have a *Head Master*; St Paul's School and Manchester Grammar School have a *High Master*; King Edward's School, Birmingham, has a *Chief Master*; Dulwich, Haileybury and Marlborough have a *Master*. The correct form is given in the *Independent Schools Year Book*. Use the colloquial *head* only in headlines; and note that *head teacher* is two words except when part of the designated title

heads of state when these are royals, such as King Abdullah of Jordan, after the first mention refer to them as *the King* (cap). The cap at subsequent mentions applies only to overseas heads of state and the British Royal Family, eg, Prince B. of Thailand (a minor royal) would become *the prince* thereafter. See **Royal Family**, **Titles** special section (page 189)

healthcare one word

heartbroken, heartbreaking, heartfelt, heartstrings, but hyphenate *heart-rending*, *heart-throb*

Heathrow sufficiently well-known not to need airport in title. Note at Heathrow, *Terminal 1, 2, 3, 4, 5* etc. See **airports**, **Gatwick**

Heaven, Hell cap in religious context only; see **Devil**

heavenly bodies cap the proper names of planets, stars, constellations etc: *Venus, Arcturus, the Plough, Aries*; for comets, l/c the word comet in, for example, *Halley's comet*. The Sun, the Moon, the Earth, the Universe are capped in their planetary or astronomical sense (see **Earth**). Use l/c for the adjectives *lunar* and *solar*, but cap *Martian* both adjectivally and as a noun

Heep, Uriah (not Heap)

Hell's Angels

help to use *to* plus verb, eg, "he helped *to* make the cake" (not "he helped make the cake")

helping the police with their inquiries avoid this phrase – suspects rarely willingly help the police. Say *were being interviewed* instead

helpline one word; similarly *hotline*

hemisphere l/c northern, southern, eastern, western

heraldry do not confuse *crests* with *coats of arms*. Most arms consist of a shield and a crest; crests are the topmost part of the coat of arms (think of the crest of a bird or a wave)

Hereford and Worcester see **unitary authorities**

Heriot-Watt University, Edinburgh

Her Majesty's pleasure (as in *detained at . . .*)

Herzegovina (as in Bosnia-Herzegovina)

Heyhoe Flint, Rachael (no hyphen, not Rachel)

Hezbollah (Party of God in Iran and Lebanon); soft-hyphenate (on a break) as Hezb-ollah

Hibernian means of or concerning Ireland, not Scotland, despite the Edinburgh football club of the same name

hiccup (not hiccough)

hi-fi acceptable abbreviation, noun or adjective, of *high fidelity*

high acceptable usage as a noun, eg, *she was on a high*. But avoid clichés such as *all-time high* and *hits new high*

highbrow, lowbrow

high command avoid clichéd use, as in *Tory high command*. See **Politics** special section (page 181)

High Commissioner caps when specific, eg, *the Indian High Commissioner*; thereafter *the high commissioner*. Remember that Commonwealth countries and the UK have high commissioners serving in high commissions in each other's countries, not ambassadors serving in embassies. See **Ambassador**

High Court see **Courts** special section (page 176)

highfalutin

high-flyer

High Sheriff caps when specific

high street l/c and no hyphen in general sense, as in *high street prices*. But cap when specific, eg, *Putney High Street*

high-tech adjective; spell out in text, but *hi-tech* is acceptable in headlines

hike never use in the American sense of a *rise* or *to raise* (rates etc); permissible only in direct quotes, or in context of walking (hitch-hike etc)

Hinckley, Leicestershire but note *Hinkley Point*, Somerset

Hindi for language contexts (the Hindi language); but use *Hindu* for religious and ethnic contexts (an adherent to Hinduism, or relating to Hinduism)

hippy, hippies nowadays as old-fashioned as *beatniks*; see **Gypsy, travellers**

Hirst, Damien (artist; not Damian)

historic, historical prefer *an historic event* rather than *a historic*; see **a, an**. Also, take care with use of *historical* and *historic*; the former can refer only to past history, while the latter can refer to a contemporary event likely to be of long-term significance. But *an historic building* is now in common usage as a synonym of an old building

hit avoid in text in sense of *affected*, eg, "Homeowners were hit last night by an interest rate rise", or in the sense of attack, eg, "The minister hit out at his critics". Sparing use of the verb in headlines is permissible

hitch-hiker, hitch-hiking etc

Hitchin, Hertfordshire (not Hitchen)

hitlist, hitman now no hyphens

HIV is a virus, not a disease. Do not write *HIV virus* (tautology), but use a phrase such as *HIV-infected*. See **Aids**

hoards (stocks or stores of treasure, for example); note *to hoard* (to amass and store food, money etc); never confuse with **hordes** (large groups or gangs of wild beasts etc)

Hogmanay cap

holidaymaker one word

Holland, now use **The Netherlands** for all contexts except sports teams or historical uses, or when referring to the provinces of North or South Holland. The adjective is *Dutch*

Holy Communion caps; see **Christian terms**

Holy Grail caps

Holyroodhouse see **Palace of Holyroodhouse**

homebuyers, homeowners no hyphens

home town (two words), but hyphenate in adjectival use, eg, *home-town memories*

Home Counties, the caps

homoeopathy (not the American homeopathy)

homogeneous means having parts all of the same kind; *homogenous*

means similar owing to common descent

Homo sapiens see **scientific names**

homosexual see **gay**

Hon, the normally use this form of address (the Hon So-and-So) only on the Court Page

Hong Kong but note *Hongkong and Shanghai Banking Corporation (HSBC)*. Until July 1, 1997, when Britain handed the colony over to China, Hong Kong had a *Governor* (cap). See **Midland**

honours people are *appointed* Privy Counsellor, Baronet, KBE, CBE, OBE, MBE etc; never say they were made, received, were awarded, or got the OBE etc. *Peers* and above (viscounts etc) are *created*, not appointed etc. At investitures, those honoured receive the insignia of the award, not the award itself. Normally omit honours and decorations after names, but the following can be used where relevant: KG, KT, VC, GC, OM, CH, MP, QC, RA, FRS etc. See **Titles** special section (page 189)

honours lists see **New Year Honours**

Hoover trade name, so cap; generally use *vacuum cleaner* and *to vacuum*

hopefully try to avoid in the sense of *it is hoped that,* even though this usage is widespread

Horse Guards Parade

horse race/racing two words, but *racing* alone is preferable. Note *Horserace Betting Levy Board*; see **racecours**e, **Sports** special section (page 185)

horticulturist (not horticulturalist)

hospitalise, hospitalisation always avoid these Americanisms; use *taken to hospital* etc

host avoid using as a verb as in "Arsenal will host Aston Villa on Saturday"; use *play host to* instead. But note a *person* can *host* an event

hotline one word; similarly *helpline*

hotpants one word

hoummos see **taramasalata**

housebuilder, housebuilding but note *the House-Builders' Federation*

however when used in the sense of *nevertheless*, always place a comma after it (and before, when in the middle of a sentence, eg, "It was said, however, that the agent . . .")

Hubble Space Telescope

Hudson Bay but note *Hudson's Bay Company*

human beings rather than just humans

human rights European Convention on Human Rights; European Court of Human Rights; the now-defunct European Commission of Human Rights; all established under the aegis of the Council of Europe, not the EU (or EC). See **Courts** special section (page 176)

humorist (not humourist)

Humphrys, John (radio and TV); but note Barry Humphries (Dame Edna Everage etc)

Hussein, King the late King of Jordan, not *Husain*; similarly, President Saddam Hussein (Iraq)

Hutus, Tutsis note plural of the Rwandan tribes (not simply Hutu, Tutsi)

hyphens generally be sparing with hyphens and run together words where the sense suggests and where they look familiar; eg, *blacklist, businessman, goldmine, knockout, intercontinental, motorcycle, takeover,* and *walkover*. Unusual hyphenations are listed separately in this guide. However, a few guidelines can be specified:
    a. usually run together prefixes except where the last letter of the prefix is the same as the first letter of the word to which it attaches: *prearrange, postwar, prewar, nonconformist*; but *pre-empt, co-ordinate, co-operate, re-establish*
    b. hyphenate composites where the same two letters come together, eg, *film-makers*, but an exception should be made when double *r* occurs in the middle: *override, overrule* (not *over-ride* etc), and note *granddaughter* and *goddaughter*
    c. generally do not use dangling hyphens, eg, *full and part-time employment* etc; this does not apply to prefixes, eg, *pre- or post-match drinks*
    d. for hyphenation when qualifying adjectives, see **adverbs**
    e. always use a hyphen rather than a slash in dates etc, eg, 1982–83 (not 1982/83)

I...

IATA International Air Transport Association; all caps

ice-cream hyphen, similarly *ice-lolly*; see also **Häagen-Dazs**

Identikit proprietary term, so cap; but note l/c *photofit*

ie use comma either side. See **eg**

ill-health hyphen; similarly *ill-feeling, ill-intentioned* etc

Immigration Service caps; similarly *Prison Service, Probation Service*

impacted on avoid this Americanism

imply see **infer**

impostor (not imposter)

impresario

Impressionist, Post-Impressionist see **artistic movements**

in addition to prefer *as well as* or *besides*

inadmissible (not -able)

include do not confuse with *comprise*: "breakfast includes toast and coffee", but "breakfast comprises cereals, toast, butter, marmalade and coffee" (ie, where the full list of elements is given)

incommunicado

indestructible (not -able)

index plural is *indices*, but note *indexes* for books

indispensable (not -ible)

Indo-China

Industrial Revolution, the use caps

industrial tribunals these no longer exist; they are now *employment tribunals*. They end with a *judgment* or a *decision*, not a verdict. Only juries in court hearings, or magistrates hearing cases summarily, deliver a verdict. Note that *immigration adjudicators* and *immigration appeal tribunals* deliver *determinations*. See **Courts** special section (page 176)

inevitable do not use as a synonym of *customary, usual* or *predictable*

in fact can almost invariably be omitted

infer do not confuse with *imply*: to *infer* is to draw a conclusion from a suggestion, to imply is to make the suggestion. A useful mnemonic: we *imply* things when we speak, we *infer* things when we listen

infighting one word, but note hyphen with *in-house*

infra-red

initials where familiar, no need to spell out at first mention (eg, BBC, TUC, Nato etc). Otherwise, usually give name in full followed by initials in parentheses, and the abbreviated form thereafter (though sometimes a word such as *the organisation* or *the group* will be preferable to avoid a mass of initials in the same story). Also, with a body as well known as the UN, it would be absurd to write the United Nations (UN), so use discretion.

Where the initials can be spoken as a word, write them as upper and lower case, eg, Nato, Gatt, Unesco, Efta – but there are some important exceptions to this, eg, MORI, IATA, RADA, RIBA, SANE, MIND, BUPA and AXA

With people's names, put points between the initials (with thin space between), though omit points in names of firms such as WH Smith, J Sainsbury

injure, injury implies something more serious than *hurt*. Avoid writing "John *received* an injury" – instead use *suffered* or *sustained* an injury, or (simply) *was injured*. Injured or sick people should not be described as *satisfactory* or *critical* – it is their *condition* that is satisfactory etc

Inland Revenue subsequent mentions, *the Revenue* (cap). See **taxman**

innocent take great care with this word, and avoid phrases such as *the innocent victim of the attack* and clichés such as *innocent children*. Best to stick to its literal sense of *not guilty*

innocuous

Inns of Court the order of precedence among the Inns is Lincoln's Inn, Inner Temple, Middle Temple, Gray's Inn

inoculate

inpatients, outpatients no hyphen

inquests see **coroner's court**

inquire, inquiry (not enquire, enquiry). But note the exception, *Directory Enquiries*

insignia plural; see **honours**

install but note *instalment*

instil

Institute of Contemporary Arts ("of" not "for" and plural Arts)

Institute of Directors IoD acceptable for headings and occasionally in text, though prefer *the institute* after first mention in full

insure you *insure* against risk; you *assure* your life; *ensure* means to make certain

Intelligence cap as a noun in the context of the security services, eg, "he was in British Intelligence", but l/c adjectival uses, eg, "she was interviewed by intelligence officers"

intelligentsia

intensive do not confuse with *intense* or *extreme*. It means concentrated, as in *intensive care*

InterCity (rail); but note adjective *inter-city*

interdependence

interesting avoid as an adjective in text; let the reader decide

interest rate cuts/rises no hyphens; never use *hikes* for *rises*

inter-governmental conference (EU's continuing discussions on the single currency etc); IGC as abbreviation. See **Maastricht**

International Atomic Energy Agency (never Authority); abbreviate to IAEA

International Olympic Committee (not Olympics); IOC as abbreviation. See **Olympics**

Internazionale (Milan football club); must not be called Inter Milan. It can be shortened to *Inter*; the other big club in the city is *AC Milan* (shortened to *Milan*)

Internet, the cap; use *the Net* (cap) for short. See **World Wide Web**

interpretative (not interpretive)

interred (buried); do not confuse with *interned* (imprisoned)

intifada (religious struggle or uprising); l/c and roman

inverted commas should be used as sparingly as possible in text: eg, unnecessary in constructions such as *he described the book as "turgid"*.

They are no longer used with works of art. See also **italics, quotation marks**

Iran use Persia only in historical context; note the language is *Farsi*, not Iranian or Persian

irascible (not irrascible)

Ireland the two parts should be called the *Republic of Ireland* or the *Irish Republic* (avoid Eire except in direct quotes or historical context), and *Northern Ireland* or *Ulster*. Do not use the phrase the Six Counties. Other important styles:

   a. *loyalist* with l/c *l* and no quotes – to balance *republican* and *nationalist*

   b. *Unionist, Unionism* (caps)

   c. *the North, the South* (caps in this specific Irish context)

   d. similarly *the Republic, the Province*

   e. *the Troubles*

   f. *the Garda* (the police force; but note *garda/gardai* for policeman/policemen); but the phrase *Irish police* is acceptable

   g. *Londonderry*, but Derry City Council; and Derry when in direct quotes or in a specifically republican context (this latter rarely)

   h. *West Belfast, East Belfast* (caps because of clearly defined sectarian areas); but north Belfast, south Belfast (unspecific, directional); note Shankill Road (not Shankhill)

   i. *Downing Street declaration*

   j. *Anglo-Irish agreement*

   k. *Frameworks for the Future*, or *the framework document* (l/c) for the Anglo-Irish proposals of February 1995

   l. *Northern Ireland Assembly*, with cap for *Assembly*

   m. avoid *Provos* as synonym of the Provisional IRA, except in quotes

   n. *Taoiseach* is an acceptable alternative for Irish Prime Minister

   o. Irish counties should be written as *Co Donegal, Co Down* etc

   p. *Orange Order, Orangemen* (caps)

iridescent (not irr-)

Iron Curtain

ironic beware of misuse. It means using or displaying irony, or in the nature of irony; it does not mean strange or paradoxical

irreconcilable

irresistible (not -able)

Isa(s) individual savings account(s), l/c; hyphenate *mini-Isas, maxi-*

I

Isas. See also **Tessa(s), Pep(s)**

-ise, -isation avoid the *z* construction in almost all cases, eg, *apologise, organise, emphasise, televise.* But note *capsize, synthesizer*

ISIS Independent Schools Information Service (not Isis)

Islam (religion of the Muslims); *Islamic* is interchangeable with *Muslim* as the adjective, though normally use Islamic with religion and fundamentalism, Muslim with architecture, politics etc

Israeli (native of Israel); *Israelite* refers to Ancient Israel

italics avoid in headlines and use sparingly in text. However, there are certain guidelines for using italics:

    a. all works of art, even where quotation marks used to be used, including titles of books, long and short poems, short stories, newspapers (see separate list under **newspapers**), magazines, pamphlets, chapter headings, White Papers, Green Papers, official reports and studies, programmes on radio and television, films, plays, computer games, musical works including operas, songs, hymns, album titles etc (see **musical vocabulary**), paintings, drawings, sculptures, titles of exhibitions. See **Arts** special section (page 176)

    b. less common, non-Anglicised foreign words go in italics, but err on the side of roman (eg, in extremis, hors d'oeuvre, angst); see foreign words

    c. names of ships, aircraft, locomotives etc

    d. a word may be italicised for emphasis, but again be sparing with this device

ITN never write ITN news; see **television**

ITV acceptable alternative for *independent television*; see **television**

J...

Jacuzzi trade name, so cap; use *whirlpool bath* if in doubt

jail, jailer (not gaol, gaoler)

jargon like journalese and slang, to be strictly avoided

Jedda

Jeep proprietary term, so cap; use only if strictly applicable, otherwise *cross-country vehicle, small military truck* etc

Jehovah's Witness(es)

Jekyll and Hyde (*The Strange Case of Dr Jekyll and Mr Hyde,* by R.L.Stevenson)

Jerusalem l/c for east/west Jerusalem

jet lag two words

jetliner avoid; write *airliner* or simply *jet*

jet ski two words as noun; note hyphen with verb *to jet-ski*

jeweller, jewellery

jibe avoid this spelling; see **gibe**

jihad (holy war); roman, l/c

jobcentre takes l/c in general sense, but cap as in *Runcorn Jobcentre*

jobseeker's allowance

job titles the general rule is to cap the most senior high-profile jobs at first mention, and thereafter l/c. Thus cap at first mention Archbishop and church titles, senior civil servants, diplomatic and political leaders, civic leaders, Editor (of well-known leading publications), Director-General (of the BBC, CBI etc), Vice-Chancellor and academic titles, Chief Constable and police ranks, military titles, President of a small number of high-profile national institutions (eg, President of the Law Society, the TUC etc) and then – usually – l/c thereafter.

However, *chairman, director, managing director* (of a company), *general secretary* (of a union), *artistic director* (of a theatre) etc are l/c; as are most presidents and chairmen of societies and institutions. A certain amount of discretion is needed in this difficult area

jodhpurs

John le Carré

John o'Groat's

Johns Hopkins University, Baltimore

Joint Chiefs of Staff (US)

Jones, Vinnie (footballer; not Vinny)

Jonsson, Ulrika

joyrider no hyphen, but use as little as possible as the term can give offence; an alternative could be *young car thief*

JP (Justice of the Peace), acceptable alternative for *non-stipendiary magistrate*; see **magistrates' courts**

jubilee strictly a fiftieth anniversary, though Queen Victoria had a golden and a diamond one; so the word can be used as a periodic celebration, especially of royalty. Note *Jubilee Line* (caps) on the London Underground

Judaea (not Judea)

judges' names all circuit judges and below (ie, those in Crown Courts, in county courts, and district judges) must now always include their first name at first mention. Thus, write *Judge Fred Potts* at first mention, subsequently *Judge Potts* or simply *the judge.*

First names will not normally be necessary with High Court judges unless there are two or more with the same surname, where again it will be essential to differentiate.

The failure to identify a judge correctly can lead to complaints, corrections and even the payment of substantial damages.

In the High Court, Mr Justice X should be referred to this way throughout a story (or simply the judge) – never as Judge X. Be careful not to confuse a judge in the Court of Appeal (a Lord Justice of Appeal) with a law lord of the House of Lords, the most senior judges, who are Lords of Appeal in Ordinary (such as Lord Nolan and Lord Hoffmann).

Note designation of Lady Justice Butler-Sloss.

See **Courts** special section (page 176)

judging by one of the most frequently misused unrelated (or disconnected) participle constructions. Remember, the phrase must have a related subject to follow (I, we, she etc). A convenient alternative is "to judge from ..." (eg, "Judging by this film, the country is in a mess" is wrong; "To judge from this film, the country is in a mess" is correct; so is "Judging by this film, we conclude that the country is in a mess"). See **participles**

judgment (not judgement)

jukebox (no hyphen)

jump-jet hyphen; but note *jumbo jet* (no hyphen)

junior abbreviate to *Jr* (not Jnr) in the American context, eg, John Eisendorf Jr; see **senior**

Justices' Clerks' Society note two apostrophes

juvenile courts no longer exist; they are now called *youth courts*. See **Courts** special section (page 176)

K...

k avoid for 1,000 except in direct quotes

kaftan but note *cagoule*

Kant, Immanuel (not Emmanuel)

Karajan, Herbert von; thereafter just Karajan (not von Karajan)

Karpov, Anatoly note also Kasparov, Garry. See **chess names, Russian names**

Kathmandu

Kellogg's Corn Flakes but *cornflakes* (generic)

kerosene (American for paraffin)

Kevorkian, Dr Jack (the American euthanasia doctor; not Kervorkian)

Kfor, the Nato-led force in Kosovo (not KFOR)

Khan Imran Khan and Jemima Khan are happy to be known as Mr Khan and Mrs Khan respectively after first mention. Imran is permissible on its own in headlines. But in most cases, beware of Khan as the family name: it is usually a title given to officials or rulers in Central Asia

Khartoum

Khashoggi, Soraya, Adnan etc

Khmer Rouge (Cambodian faction); note a *Khmer* is a Cambodian

Khrushchev, Nikita

kick-off noun; but note *to kick off*

kick-start hyphenate, noun or verb

killer can be used for *murderer* but do not use *assassin* as a synonym

kilogram (not kilogramme); see **gram, metric**

kilometres per hour correct abbreviation is *km/h* rather than kph

kilowatt-hour correct abbreviation is *kWh*. The cost of generating electricity at a power station is usually expressed in pence per kilowatt-hour (*2.9p/kWh*). See **megawatts**

King's College London apostrophe, no commas

King's Cross, London

King's Lynn, Norfolk

Kings Road, Chelsea (do not use apostrophe)

Kingston upon Hull official name for Hull; normally just use Hull. Note that Humberside no longer exists as a local authority; see **unitary authorities**

Kingston upon Thames no hyphens; use *southwest London* rather than Surrey; but note that Surrey County Council is still based in Kingston. See **postal addresses**

kitchen cabinet l/c *cabinet* in this informal context. See **Cabinet**

Kitemark see **British Standards Institution**

kneejerk (reaction etc); no hyphen, but beware of overuse

knockout noun; but note *to knock out*

knowhow one word as noun

knowledgeable

Knox-Johnston, (Sir) Robin (yachtsman)

Kodak trade name, so cap

Koh-i-noor (diamond)

Koran, the cap and roman, like the Bible

Korean names note all initial caps and no hyphens, eg, Roh Tae Woo

Kosovo, Kosovan do not use Kosova, Kosovar

kowtow no hyphen

Ku Klux Klan no longer use hyphens

KwaZulu/Natal (not Natal/KwaZulu); see **South Africa**

Kyrgyzstan (no longer Kirghizia)

L...

Labor Day (US); no equivalent in UK so retain US spelling; Anglicise the *Defence Department* etc

Labor Party (Australia)

Labour Party (UK); abbreviate in lists etc to *Lab*. See **Politics** special section (page 181)

Ladbrokes (betting shop); but *Ladbroke plc*; note also *William Hill* and *Coral* (neither takes final *s*)

lady, ladies prefer *woman, women*

Lafite, Château- see **wines**

Lagos, Nigeria (note Abuja is the capital of Nigeria)

laissez faire no longer use *laisser* version

Lake District do not include *Lake* when the name contains its equivalent; thus Windermere, Derwent Water, but Lake Bassenthwaite

lambast (not lambaste)

lamé use accent to distinguish it from *lame*

lamppost no hyphen

Land Rover no hyphen; similarly *Range Rover*

Land's End

landmine no hyphen

landslide (political); but *landslip* (earth)

languor, languorous (not -our)

laptop (computer), no hyphen; note also *desktop*

largesse (not largess)

last, past *last* should not be used as a synonym of *latest*; "the last few days" means the *final* few days; "the past few days" means the *most recent* few days

Last Post like Reveille, is *sounded* (not played)

Latin be sparing in its use, apart from in the Law Report. When Latin phrases are in common usage, use roman rather than italics, eg, quid pro quo, QED, ex parte injunction, habeas corpus

Latin dancing cap Latin in this and all other contexts, eg, *the Latin language*, *Latin music*, *Latin temperament* etc

latitude, longitude write 45° 32'N, 40° 17'W etc

La traviata note l/c *t*

launderette (not laundrette)

Lautro Life Assurance and Unit Trust Regulatory Organisation

law lords, law officers l/c; see **judges**, **Courts** special section (page 176)

lawnmower one word

Law Report in *The Times*, always initial caps and singular (not Reports); so the style for x-refs is bold, right, eg, **Law Report, page 42**

lay, lie a person *lays* a carpet (transitive verb), but *lies* on a carpet (intransitive). Do not confuse

lay-by but note *layout*

Leader use caps for Leader of the Commons/House of Lords/Opposition; but note l/c *Labour leader*, *Tory leader* etc

lean, leap past tenses *leant*, *leapt* (not leaned, leaped)

Lea River but *Lee Valley Regional Park Authority* etc

learnt past tense and past participle of *learn*; note adjective *learned* (as in scholarly)

Lebanon (not the Lebanon, except occasionally in historical context); see **Sudan**

Lebed, Aleksandr call him General Lebed, not Mr

le Carré, John

Lecs local enterprise councils; initial cap only. See **Tecs**

Lee Kuan Yew (of Singapore)

Left, the cap in the political context when referring to a group of like-minded individuals, eg, "The Left added to Tony Blair's worries"; but l/c in "the party swung to the left". When the Left is qualified, keep the adjective l/c, eg, *the hard Left*, *the far Left*. Also *the left wing, left-wing* *contenders, leftwingers*. See **Right**

legal aid l/c and never hyphenate, even adjectivally in phrases such as *legal aid cases*. But note *Legal Aid Board*

legal terms in general, use l/c for titles etc except when in full or specific: thus, the Recorder of Liverpool (thereafter *the recorder*), the West London Magistrate, Chelmsford Crown Court, Horseferry Road Magistrates' Court (caps on first mention), etc; but "the court was told", "the judge said", "the magistrate ordered" etc.

The *Bench* is capped only when referring to the judges as a group; a *bench of magistrates* is always l/c. See **magistrates' courts**.

Always cap the *Bar* and the *Inn* (even when used on its own). See **Courts** special section (page 176)

legendary avoid its clichéd use

legionella, listeria, salmonella note all are bacteria, not viruses

legionnaires' disease

Legion of Honour or **Légion d'honneur** either form is acceptable, according to context

Le Manoir aux Quat' Saisons (restaurant)

Leonardo da Vinci at second mention always Leonardo (never da Vinci)

leper do not use as a metaphor or as an insult

lèse-majesté (treason, or insult to a monarch); note italic and accents

less use *less* for quantity, *fewer* for number; see **fewer**

lesser opposite to *greater* (eg, *the lesser evil*); not to be used as a synonym of *less*

letter bomb hyphenate only in adjectival use

letterbox, postbox no hyphens

leukaemia

Levi's (jeans) should take the apostrophe; but use *Levi Strauss* for the company

liaison, liaise the word *link* is often better. The verb *to liaise* has forced its way into the language; however, use sparingly and only in its correct sense – to establish co-operation, to act as a link with – not as a synonym of *meet* or *talk*

Liberal Democrats *Lib Dems* is an acceptable alternative in either headlines or text; do not shorten to Liberals. Abbreviate in lists etc to *LD*. See **Politics** special section (page 181)

licence noun, note **license** (verb), *licensee* (noun), *licensed, licensing*. See **practice**

Liechtenstein

lifeguard (on a beach); note *Life Guardsman* (on a horse)

lifelong one word as adjective

liferaft one word; similarly *lifeboat, lifebelt* etc

lifesize(d) no hyphen

lift-off (spacecraft etc); similarly *take-off*

lightning (as in electrical storm); *lightening* (as in making lighter)

light-year

like do not use as a synonym of *such as* (eg, write "cities such as Manchester are ambitious", not "cities like Manchester . . . "); nor as a synonym of *as if* (eg, write "he looks as if he is succeeding", not "he looks like he is succeeding")

likeable

lily of the valley

linchpin (not lynchpin)

liner take care with this word, which strictly no longer applies to passenger cruise ships. Liners nowadays are cargo vessels trading regularly between designated ports, eg, container ships. Confine use of *liner* for passenger ships to historical contexts, eg, the transatlantic liner *Queen Mary*

line-up noun; but note verb *to line up*

Lipizzaner horses (do not use Lippizaner)

liquefy (not liquify); but note *to liquidate*

liquorice (not the American licorice)

lira (Italian currency) singular; note the plural *lire*

literally avoid as expression of emphasis: "he literally exploded with anger" is absurd

livery halls (City of London) note no definite article (eg, Drapers' Hall, not the Drapers' Hall); see **London**

living room no hyphen as *dining room* etc

Livingstone, Ken, Dr David Livingstone (explorer), but *Livingston*, West Lothian

Livorno, rather than *Leghorn*, despite usual style of Anglicising foreign names

Lloyds TSB, the bank, but **Lloyd's of London** (insurance)

Lloyd's names (not Names)

Lloyd-Webber use hyphen for Lord L-W, but no hyphen for brother Julian

loan noun (ie, never say "I loaned him £20" etc); the verb is *lend/lent*

loathe (verb); note the adjective *loath* (not loth)

local government cap councils when full title, eg, Watford Borough Council, Newtown District Council (thereafter the council); but l/c when title is not in full, eg, Watford council; use l/c for all council committees; cap Mayor at first mention (eg, Albert Hobart, Mayor of Rochdale), l/c for council officials such as *borough surveyor, town clerk*; cap the seat of local government if we are sure of its title (eg, Leeds City Hall, Birmingham Council House – not to be confused with Birmingham Town Hall – Lambeth Town Hall)

lochs (Scotland); note *loughs* (Ireland)

Lockerbie suspects the two accused are Abdul Baset Ali al-Megrahi (after first mention, al-Megrahi); and Lamin Khalifa Fhimah (thereafter Fhimah)

lockout (in industrial disputes etc), one word; but *to lock out*

locomotive names italicise, as with ships' or aircraft names, eg, *Mallard*. Do not use *the* unless certain it is part of the name. See **aircraft names, ships**

London cap the *East End* and the *West End* of London, and now also *North London, South London, East London* and *West London, Central London, Inner London*; but l/c *southeast London, southwest London* etc. The local council for the City of London is the Court of Common Council, whose members are common councilmen; cap Borough in titles of particular boroughs, eg, London Borough of Bromley; see **livery halls**

London Clinic, The cap *T*

London clubs note particularly *the Athenaeum*; *Boodle's*; *Brooks's*;

Buck's Club; *Pratt's Club*; *the Queen's Club*; *Royal Over-Seas League*; *Savile Club*; *Travellers Club*; *United Oxford and Cambridge University Club*; *White's Club*. It would be wrong to say, eg, Boodle's Club; on the other hand, it is permissible to refer to the Garrick Club, the Reform Club, the Savage Club etc simply as the Garrick, the Reform or the Savage

Londonderry see **Ireland**

London hotels, restaurants as with London clubs, it is essential to give the correct form of the following: *Berkeley Hotel*; *Brown's Hotel*; *Claridge's*; *the Dorchester*; *Four Seasons hotel*; *Grosvenor House*; *Hilton International Kensington*; *Hyatt Carlton Tower hotel*; *Hyde Park Hotel*; *The Lanesborough*; *Langham Hilton*; *Le Meridien Piccadilly*; *London Hilton on Park Lane*; *Marriott Hotel*; *New Connaught Rooms*; *Park Lane Hotel*; *Quaglino's*; *Ritz Hotel*; *Savoy Hotel*; *Simpson's-in-the-Strand*; *Waldorf Hotel*; *Westmoreland Hotel*

London Zoo cap *Zoo*

Longchamp (French racecourse; not Longchamps)

longstanding no longer use hyphen

lookout noun, no hyphen

Lord Advocate do not add *for Scotland*

Lord Chancellor's Department caps, and not Lord Chancellor's Office

Lord Mayor caps, as in Lord Mayor of London, Birmingham etc; thereafter *the lord mayor*; the same applies to Mayor of Guildford etc

Lord's (cricket ground)

lords justices both words take the plural

lord-lieutenant should be hyphenated, according to the Association of Lord-Lieutenants (note this plural, not lords-lieutenant); use l/c in general use, but the Lord-Lieutenant of Gloucestershire etc (when specific)

lorry prefer *lorry* to the American *truck*, but truck has become ubiquitous and cannot be banned, especially from foreign stories

loss-maker, loss-making

loveable note the middle *e*; similarly *likeable*

lowbrow similarly *highbrow*

Lower House, Upper House (of Parliament); see **Politics** special section (page 181)

M

low-key

loyalist see **Ireland**

Ltd can usually be dropped from company names (as can plc)

lullaby (not -bye)

lumbar as in the lower back (eg, *lumbar puncture*); note *lumber* as in junk furniture, lumberjacks, or (verbally) moving clumsily about etc

Lusta (not Lusa), in Skye, often quoted as the wettest place in the UK

Luton airport note l/c airport; resist pressure to insert *international*. See **airports**

Luxembourg (not -burg); the inhabitants should be called Mr, Mrs etc, rather than M or Mme (see **foreign appellations**, and **Santer**); but note *Rosa Luxemburg* (leader of Berlin uprising in 1919)

Lycra proprietary term, so cap

Lyons (not Lyon); see **Marseilles, foreign places**

-lyse the style is *analyse*, *paralyse* etc (not -ize); see **-ise, -isation**

Lytham St Anne's, Lancashire (note apostrophe, but no hyphens)

Lyttelton Theatre (at the National); similarly, Humphrey Lyttelton (jazz musician)

M...

M1 (do not write M1 motorway)

Maastricht treaty l/c *treaty*, but note *Treaty of Maastricht*; for an unofficial name for the updated version of the treaty, write *Maastricht II* (not 2 or Two). See **inter-governmental conference**

Macau (not Macao)

Mac, Mc always check spelling of these prefixes in *Who's Who*; in alphabetical lists, treat Mc as Mac

McCarthy, Senator Joseph note *McCarthyism*

McCartney, (Sir) Paul

MacDonald, Ramsay

McDonald, Trevor (newsreader)

McDonald's (hamburger chain)

McDonnell Douglas no hyphen

MacDowell, Andie

Macedonia the correct (and politically sensitive) title of the new republic is the Former Yugoslav Republic of Macedonia (caps as shown). See **Yugoslav**

Machiavelli(an)

machinegun but note *sub-machinegun*

mackintosh (raincoat)

Mackintosh, (Sir) Cameron

MacLaine, Shirley

Maclean, Donald

McLuhan, Marshall

Macmillan, Harold same spelling for the publishers

Macpherson, Elle

macroeconomic, microeconomic no hyphen

Macy's (New York store)

Madame Tussaud's

"mad cow" disease see **BSE, Creutzfeldt-Jakob disease**

Madejski Stadium, Reading (not Madjeski)

Madison Square Garden, New York (not Gardens)

maestros (not maestri); plural of *maestro*

Mafia cap only in Italian or US context; l/c *mafia* in countries such as Russia when used as a synonym of gangsters

Mafikeng, the new name (since 1980) of Mafeking. Spell according to historical context

Magdalen College, Oxford; but note *Magdalene College,* Cambridge. See **Oxford University, Cambridge University**

Maghreb see **Middle East**

magistrates' courts caps for *the Metropolitan Magistrate, West London Magistrate* etc, but usually magistrates take l/c. An acceptable alternative for a non-stipendiary (ie, lay) magistrate is JP (Justice of the Peace). When the accused is appearing before the bench, he appears before the magistrates (plural) unless a stipendiary magistrate, who usually sits on his own. The full name of the court is capped, as in *Bow Street Magistrates' Court*. See **courts, legal terms, Courts** special section (page 176)

Magna Carta (not *the* Magna Carta)

MAID (not Maid); now renamed Dialog Corporation

mailshot

major do not use as a lazy alternative for *big, chief, important* or *main*

Majorca, Minorca use the Anglicised forms. See **Spanish regions**

majority of do not use as alternative for *most of*

makeover one word as noun; but try to avoid this cliché – use *remodelling* instead

make-up (cosmetics or typography; not makeup)

Malaysia Datuk Seri Dr Mahathir Mohamad, the Prime Minister; thereafter Dr Mahathir

Mall, The note cap *T*

management buyout spell out first time, though MBO is acceptable on Business pages

manifestos (not -oes)

Manila (capital of the Philippines)

manoeuvre, manoeuvring, manoeuvrable

mantelpiece (not mantlepiece)

manuscript(s) write out when part of a sentence, but abbreviate to MSS when quotation from catalogue, or in headline if context is clear

Mao Zedong (no longer Mao Tse-tung); see **Chinese names**

marathon avoid in clichéd sense of *a long time* as in "a marathon session"

march past noun; two words in military context

Mardi Gras, the Shrove Tuesday festival; but note the self-styled *Mardi Gra bomber*

Margrethe, Queen of Denmark (not Margarethe)

Marines cap in both *Royal Marines* and *US Marines*; note also *a Marine*

marketplace one word; but note *market-maker*

Marks & Spencer use the ampersand rather than *and* in text; can abbreviate to M&S in headlines; the formal legal title is *Marks and Spencer plc*, but this form is used only rarely

marquess (not marquis, except in foreign titles). See **Titles** special section (page 189)

Marrakesh (not Marrakech)

married couple's allowance

Marseilles (not Marseille); call the football club *Marseilles* (not Olympique de Marseille)

Martini trade name, so cap

Marxist, Marxism derived from Karl Marx, so cap. Do not use as loose variant of communism; see **communism**

Mary Celeste (not *Marie Celeste*)

Mass cap in its religious context; note also *Holy Mass* and *Requiem Mass*. See **Churches** special section (page 172)

Massachusetts

massive avoid as a synonym of *big*

MasterCard

masterclass (musical etc); no hyphen

master of foxhounds l/c; see **foxhunt**

Master of the Queen's Music

Master of the Rolls see **Courts** special section (page 176)

Matabele singular and plural – *a Matabele, the Matabele*

materialise avoid as a synonym of *appear, come about* or *happen*

mathematics spell out in text, though maths acceptable in direct quotes and headlines

Mathews, Meg (married to Noel Gallagher)

matinee no accent; similarly *premiere, debut, decor* etc. See **Arts**

special section (page 169)

matins l/c; see **evensong, Christian terms**

Maupassant, Guy de

Mauretania (liner); note **Mauritania** (country)

may/might do not confuse; use *might* in sentences referring to past possibilities that did not happen, eg, "If that had happened ten days ago, my whole life might have been different". A clear distinction is evident in the following: "He might have been captured by the Iraqis – but he wasn't", compared with "He may have been captured by the Iraqis – it is possible but we don't know"

Maya, one of the Indian people of Central America; *Mayas*, plural; and *Mayan*, adjective

mayday (SOS call) l/c; but note *May Day* (holiday)

Mayfair but note *May Fair Hotel*

mayor for when to cap, see **local government, Lord Mayor**

Maze prison, Northern Ireland use Long Kesh only in historical context

MCC do not write *the MCC*. See **Sports** special section (page 185)

mealtimes write *breakfast time, lunchtime, teatime, dinner time, supper time* (but use hyphens in compounds when adjectival)

means-test, means-tested etc (hyphenate whether as noun, verb or adjective)

means to an end singular; but note "his means *are* modest"

Médecins sans Frontières

media plural as in *mass media*; but note *mediums* (spiritualists)

medical officer of health MoH acceptable in headlines

medical terms never use these (*geriatric, paralytic, schizophrenic* etc) metaphorically or as terms of abuse

In words ending in *-tomy* (*appendectomy, hysterectomy* etc), the word "operation" is tautologous and must not be used. See also **bacteria, X-ray**

medieval (not mediaeval)

Mediterranean

meet never use *meet with*

mega- be very sparing with this as a colloquial prefix meaning *big*

megawatts the capacity of a power station is measured in *megawatts*; the output is measured in *megawatt hours*. The correct abbreviation of megawatt is *MW* (not mW, which means milliwatt). See **kilowatt-hour**

mêlée

Member of Parliament cap *Member*, but MP almost always preferable

mementoes (not -os)

memoirs (not memoires)

memorandum plural *memorandums* (not -a)

meningitis distinguish whether bacterial or viral; the headline cases are usually bacterial

Mercedes-Benz hyphen

Merchant Navy caps

Merchant Taylors' School, Middlesex and Liverpool

Merthyr Tydfil (South Wales unitary authority) never shorten to Merthyr, which is a village in Carmarthenshire. See **unitary authorities**

Messerschmitt (not -schmidt)

mete out (in context of punishment; not meet out)

metres (as in distance, poetry etc); note *meters* (as in gas, electricity or parking etc)

metric in general non-scientific contexts continue to use the non-metric forms (miles rather than kilometres, pounds rather than kilograms, pints rather than litres). In sporting, foreign, engineering and scientific stories it will often be better to use the metric.

However, with petrol and fuel now sold in litres rather than gallons, it will be essential to give both measurements, eg, 55p a litre (£2.50 per gallon). For the foreseeable future, continue to give fuel consumption in miles per gallon, but also metric conversion in brackets at first mention.

With foodstuffs, such as cheese, prefer the metric first with the imperial conversion where practicable, though a conversion every time in a long list is unnecessary

Metropolitan Police see **Commissioner**; note also *Metropolitan Magistrate* (see **magistrates' courts**)

Michelangelo

microchip

microgram do not abbreviate, and certainly not to mcg, meaningless under international scientific standard abbreviations. The l/c *m* stands for *milli-* as a prefix. So *mg* is correct for *milligram*

mid-air hyphenate, noun or adjective

midday, midweek no hyphens

Middle Ages, the caps

Middle East comprises Bahrain, Cyprus, Egypt, Iran, Iraq, Israel, Jordan, Kuwait, Lebanon, Oman, Qatar, Saudi Arabia, Sudan, Syria, Turkey, United Arab Emirates, Yemen. In a general sense, it also takes in the countries of the Maghreb: Algeria, Libya, Mauritania, Morocco, Tunisia, Western Sahara. Never abbreviate to the Americanism Mideast

Middle England caps, in political context

Middlesbrough

Middlesex no longer a county. See **postal addresses**

Mideast unacceptable as abbreviation of Middle East

Mid Glamorgan no longer exists as a local government authority, but name persists in some organisations' titles, eg, Mid Glamorgan Tec. Note no hyphen. See **unitary authorities**

Midland Bank no longer exists as a trading entity. It is now part of *HSBC*, so use *Midland* only in historical contexts. See **Hong Kong**

midlife crisis but do not overuse this cliché

midnight (not 12 midnight); see **noon**

midsummer, midwinter

Midwest (US)

MiG (former Soviet aircraft)

migrant do not use in place of *emigrant* or *immigrant*. It means one who is in the process of migrating

mileage

military ranks use hyphens in compounds such as *Major-General*, *Lieutenant-Colonel* etc (where two ranks are joined), but not with *Second Lieutenant, Lance Corporal, Air Commodore* etc. Do not abbreviate ranks except in lists. See **Armed Forces** special section (page 164)

militate (against or in favour of); do not confuse with *mitigate*

millennium common usage says that the millennium ends on December 31, 1999, though technically it should be December 31, 2000. We should accept the former. Note caps for *the Millennium Dome* (thereafter *the Dome*), *Millennium Fund, Millennium Commission, Millennium Exhibition*. Also *Millennium Eve* (as New Year's Eve). The plural of millennium is *millennia* (unlike *memorandums* etc; see **referendum**). Note also *millenarian* (only one middle *n*) meaning of, or related to, the millennium

millions write out millions from one to ten, thereafter 11 million etc. Abbreviate to *m* only for headlines. For currencies, spell out in text, eg, £15 million, but abbreviate to £15m in headlines. With decimal notations, best to restrict to two decimal points in text, rounded up or down (eg, £1.53 million), though in headlines try to avoid decimals altogether. In text, write 2.5 million rather than two and a half million; but "three million shares changed hands" (not 3 million shares) etc

MIND the mental health charity wishes to be known thus; see **SANE**, **initials**

mind-set prefer *mentality* to this cliché

minimal do not use as a synonym of *small;* it means smallest, or the least possible in size, duration etc

miniskirt no hyphen; note also *minicab*

ministers (political) cap all ministers, whether in the Cabinet or not. The same applies to ministers in overseas governments: give name and full title (capped) first time, thereafter name or just *the minister*. See **Politics** special section (page 181)

Minnelli, Liza

minuscule (not miniscule). Originally, a medieval script. Use sparingly, as it is heavily overworked as a synonym of *very small* or *unimportant*

Mishcon de Reya (solicitors); note l/c *de*

mis-hit hyphen; similarly *mis-sell;* but note *misspell*

Miss, Ms Ms is nowadays fully acceptable when a woman (married or unmarried) wants to be called thus, or when it is not known for certain if she is Mrs or Miss. Ms is increasingly common in American contexts. See **appellations**

missing do not say *gone/went missing,* prefer *disappeared* or *vanished*

Mississippi

misspell no hyphen; see **spelt**

mitigate means to *make milder, moderating* (as in mitigating circumstances in a law case); do not confuse with *militate*

Mitterrand, François (late French President)

MoD acceptable abbreviation for *Ministry of Defence,* especially in headlines

Moët et Chandon

Mogul (not Mughal); as in empire and art

Mohammed see **Muhammad**

Moldova (no longer Moldavia)

Mona Lisa (not Monna Lisa)

monarch, the l/c for the British monarch; but note *the Sovereign, the Crown.* See **Royal Family**

Mönchengladbach (no hyphen)

Monetary Policy Committee (of the Bank of England); note caps; use MPC at subsequent mentions

moneys plural of money, but *money* will usually serve. Note also *moneyed* (not monied)

Mongol, Mongolian (race); never refer to a Down's syndrome sufferer as a mongol

Monopolies and Mergers Commission (MMC) is now renamed the *Competition Commission.* Refer to the *MMC* now only in historical context

Montagu of Beaulieu, Lord

Montenegrin is the adjective from Montenegro (not Montenegran)

months abbreviate (only in lists or listings) as follows: Jan, Feb, March, April, May, June, July, Aug, Sept, Oct, Nov, Dec

Moon cap in planetary context, otherwise l/c. See **Earth, Sun, Universe**

more than rather than *over* with numbers, eg, "more than 2,500 people attended the rally", not "over 2,500 . . ."

Moreton-in-Marsh (not Morton, nor -in-the-)

MORI must cap

Morrell, Lady Ottoline (not Otteline)

morris dancing/dancers

Morse code

mortar do not use by itself when the meaning is *mortar bomb*; the mortar is the launcher from which the shell is fired. But *mortar attack* is perfectly correct

mosquitoes (not -os as plural)

most favoured nation status

MoT certificate, test; but note otherwise *the Department of Transport*, or *Transport Department* (not Ministry of . . .)

Mother Teresa (not Theresa)

Mother's Day, or Mothering Sunday (not Mothers')

motocross (not motorcross)

motorcade acceptable for a procession of vehicles

motorcycle, motorcyclist, motorbike etc

motoring terms the following terms are appearing increasingly in the Saturday motoring pages and should be standardised: *carburettor, wheelspin, four-wheel drive* (shorten to *4WD*), but *a four-wheel-drive vehicle* (two hyphens when adjectival), *power steering, anti-lock brakes, 3-litre car, 1.9 diesel* (hyphenated when adjectival), *four-door, hatchback, four-star petrol, E-type Jaguar, Mercedes-Benz E-class* etc, *airbag, seatbelt, numberplate, sports car.*

For the foreseeable future, continue to give fuel consumption figures in miles per gallon, but also give the metric conversion in brackets at first mention. See **metric**

motor neurone disease (not neuron)

moveable keep middle *e*

movies although an Americanism, is now so common as to be an acceptable synonym of *films;* but use *films* whenever possible

MP, QC use commas each side after name. Note the plural MPs (never MP's). See **Member of Parliament, Politics** special section (page 181), **Courts** special section (page 176)

Mr, Mrs, Miss, Ms see **appellations**

mugging strictly means theft by violence in the open air. Take care not to overuse

Muhammad use this spelling for the Prophet, but respect the other spellings of the name according to individuals' preference; if in doubt, use Muhammad. Note also *Muhammad Ali*; but *King Mohammed VI* of Morocco; see **names**

Muhammad al-Masari (Saudi dissident); then Dr Masari

Mujahidin (fighters in a jihad or holy war); note cap

multi incline towards making *multi* compounds one word wherever possible, whether used as a noun or as an adjective, eg, *multimillionaire*, *multinational*, *multilateral*, *multimedia*, *multiracial*, *multispeed*, *multistorey*, *multitrack* (and note *multispeed*, *multitrack Europe*). However, hyphenate when two vowels come together, eg, multi-ethnic

multimillion-pound, multimillion-dollar as in deal etc

mum see **dad**

Murdoch, Elisabeth; refer to her as Ms Murdoch at subsequent mentions

Murdoch, Rupert at first mention he should be described as "chairman and chief executive of The News Corporation, parent company of *The Times*"

musical vocabulary
    a. *song titles* (classical or pop), *album titles*, *operas* (including arias) take italics
    b. *symphonies* take roman, caps, eg, Symphony No 3, but where symphonies have numbers and popular alternative titles, use italics, eg, *Eroica*
    c. *concertos* take roman, caps, eg, First Violin Concerto. For fuller list, see **Arts** special section (page 169)

music-hall

Muslim (not Moslem or Mohamedan); see **Islam, Muhammad**

Muzak proprietary term, so cap

Myanmar continue to call the country Burma

mynah bird prefer to mina, myna

N...

Naafi the Navy, Army and Air Force Institutes; commonly used to describe the canteen for Service personnel run by the Naafi

Nafta North American Free Trade Agreement (not Area or Association)

naive, naivety (no diaeresis)

names as a general rule, people are entitled to be known as they wish to be known, provided their identities are clear. Thus Cassius Clay became Muhammad Ali; but in such changes, give both names until the new one is widely known. Note *Lloyd's names* (l/c). See **appellations**, **Lloyd's**

names starting stories cap both names, eg, "GORDON BROWN said last night . . ." Where the name is too long to contain in the first line, reconstruct the sentence to place the name away from the start

narcotics take care to use this word correctly; see **drugs**

Nasa National Aeronautics and Space Administration (US); rarely necessary to spell out

national avoid as a synonym of *citizen,* as in *a French national*

National Air Traffic Services (caps and note plural), or the air traffic control service (informal alternative, l/c)

national anthem l/c

National Association of Schoolmasters and Union of Women Teachers full title, then abbreviate to NASUWT (no slash)

national curriculum l/c

National Health Service abbreviate to the NHS, or the health service (NHS is acceptable in headlines)

national insurance l/c, like other taxes

National Lottery caps, but usually l/c the lottery at subsequent mentions unless context unclear. Note *National Lottery Charities Board.* See **rollover**

National Parks cap, in both specific names and in general (eg, *Snowdonia National Park*; and "the policy applies particularly to National Parks")

National Rivers Authority (not River)

National Service caps

National Theatre caps; generally omit Royal. See **Lyttelton**

nationalist l/c except when referring to name of a political party. Thus *Scottish National Party* (SNP), and *Scottish Nationalists*. In Irish contexts, again l/c. See **Ireland**

nationwide no hyphen, but use sparingly as it borders on being a cliché; prefer *national* or *nationally*. See **wide**

Native American cap the N when referring to American Indians

Nato (never NATO)

NatWest acceptable abbreviation for National Westminster Bank in text or headlines

naught as in *come to naught* (not nought)

nave (central space in a church); journalists who misspell the word are *knaves*

navy, naval the Royal Navy at first mention (thereafter *the Navy*, capped); the Merchant Navy, the US Navy, the Brazilian Navy etc (thereafter *the navy*, l/c); *naval* is l/c except in titles such as Royal Naval Volunteer Reserve (RNVR) etc. See **officers**, **ships**, **warships**, **Armed Forces** special section (page 164)

Nazi, Nazism caps; see **communist**

Neanderthal (not -tal); note cap

nearby, near by the first is adjectival, eg, "the nearby school was convenient"; the second is adverbial, eg, "he sat on a bench near by"

nearly one in three ... is prefer singular to plural *are* in these constructions. See **one**

Neighbourhood Watch

Neill Committee on Standards in Public Life (headed by Lord Neill of Bladen); caps for full title

neither takes a singular verb, eg, "neither Bert nor Fred has any idea". Do not use "neither ... or" (must use nor). See **none**

nerve-racking (not -wracking); see **racked**, **wrack**

Nestlé

Netanyahu, Binyamin (Israeli politician; not Benjamin)

Net Book Agreement caps

Netherlands, The no longer interchangeable with Holland (see **Holland**)

Network SouthEast no longer exists

nevertheless one word; similarly *nonetheless*

new frequently redundant; always omit in "setting a *new* record"

New Age travellers no quotes; see **Gypsy**

newborn (as in babies); no hyphen

Newcastle upon Tyne, Newcastle-under-Lyme

New Deal caps for Labour's welfare programme; quotes at first mention if appropriate

newfound (no hyphen)

Newhaven, East Sussex but note *New Haven*, Connecticut

new Labour l/c *n*, quotes not usually necessary, except when the writer or speaker is making a particular, perhaps ironic, point. But keep caps in slogans such as *New Labour, New Danger*. See **Politics** special section (page 181)

newscaster prefer *newsreader*

News International Rupert Murdoch is chairman and chief executive of The News Corporation (second mention, News Corp). News Corp can be described as "parent company of *The Times*".

A subsidiary of News Corp is News International, a British company that owns Times Newspapers Holdings. The operating subsidiary of Times Newspapers Holdings is Times Newspapers Ltd, publisher of *The Times* and *The Sunday Times*. Times Supplements Ltd publishes the supplements – *The Times Educational Supplement, The Times Higher Education Supplement, The Times Literary Supplement* and *Nursery World* – and is a subsidiary of News International plc.

Times Newspapers Holdings is chaired by Mr Murdoch (the vice-chairman is Sir Edward Pickering) and the board includes the independent national directors of *The Times* and *The Sunday Times*. It is thus the controlling company.

News Group Newspapers, another operating subsidiary of News International, is the publisher of *The Sun* and *News of the World*.

News Ltd is the Australian arm of News Corp.

Mr Murdoch does not "own" any of these companies, though his family is the largest single (though not majority) shareholder in News Corp. See **BSkyB, Murdoch, *The Times***

newspapers/journals use italics for titles and include *The* in the title whenever appropriate. The lists that follow (source, *Willings Press Guide 1994*), though not exhaustive, should cover the most usual:

a. With *The* in the masthead: *The Times, The Sunday Times, The Sun, The Mirror* (formerly *Daily Mirror*), *The Guardian, The Independent, The Daily Telegraph, The Sunday Telegraph, The Express* (formerly *Daily Express*), *The Express on Saturday, The Observer, The Mail on Sunday, The European, The Scotsman, The Herald* (formerly *The Glasgow Herald*), *The Birmingham Post, The Journal* (Newcastle), *The Northern Echo, The Irish Times, The Spectator, The Economist, The Lancet, The Sporting Life, The Big Issue*

b. Without *The* in the masthead: *News of the World, Financial Times, Daily Mail, Daily Star, Daily Sport, Sunday Sport, Sunday Mirror, Sunday Express, Sunday People, Evening Standard, Independent on Sunday, Scotland on Sunday, Yorkshire Post, Daily Post* (Liverpool), *Manchester Evening News, Western Daily Press* (Bristol), *Western Mail* (Cardiff), *Western Morning News* (Plymouth), *Evening Argus* (Brighton), *Evening Mail* (Birmingham), *Sunday Herald* (Glasgow), *Express & Star* (Wolverhampton), *Telegraph & Argus* (Bradford), *Oxford Mail, Sunday Independent* (Dublin), *New Statesman & Society* (although just *New Statesman* is usually acceptable), *British Medical Journal* (the BMJ), *Jewish Chronicle, Which?, Which Car?* etc, *Racing Post*

c. Abroad
The Boston Globe; Chicago Tribune; Los Angeles Times; The Miami Herald; The New York Times; New York Daily News; New York Post; The New Yorker; The Washington Post; USA Today; The Wall Street Journal; International Herald Tribune; The Globe and Mail (Toronto); *Bild am Sonntag; Stern; Der Spiegel; Die Welt; Izvestia; The Times of India; El País; Le Monde; Le Figaro; L'Espresso* (Italy); *Corriere della Sera; Far Eastern Economic Review; South China Morning Post; The Straits Times* (Singapore); *New Straits Times* (Malaysia); *The Australian; The Sydney Morning Herald; The Jerusalem Post*

d. When the journal's name is used adjectivally, omit *The*, eg, "the *Times* reporter was attacked . . ."

e. Always properly attribute material from another newspaper: never say "a report in another newspaper . . ." but "a report in *The Guardian* . . ." etc. However, the general phrases *media reports* or *press reports* are acceptable when material has been widely disseminated

New Year Honours or **New Year's Honours List** caps; note also caps for *the Queen's Birthday Honours*. See **honours**

New Year's Day, New Year's Eve but note **the new year** and **Chinese new year**

New York City, New York State caps, usually *New York* is sufficient for the city; *upstate New York* is permissible. Normally, l/c *state* in contexts such as *the state of Virginia,* but see **Washington**

New Zealand (never NZ, even in headlines)

Nicolson, (Sir) Harold but note *Jack Nicholson* (actor)

Nietzsche

nightclub

nightmare use only in its proper sense of an unpleasant dream, not as a lazy cliché for something that goes wrong

night-time hyphen; but note *daytime* (one word)

Nikkei average

Nissan (cars); but note *Nissen hut*

No 10, or **10 Downing Street** (not Number 10 or Downing St); see **Downing Street, Politics** special section (page 181)

no-fly zone

no man's land

no one two words, no hyphen

"no" vote, "yes" vote

"no win, no fee" (legislation/agreement etc); see **Courts** special section (page 176)

Nobel Prize for Literature, Medicine etc; or *Nobel Peace/Literature Prize*; but note l/c for *Nobel prize* (unspecific), *Nobel prizewinner* (but *Nobel Prize-winning author*), *Nobel laureate*

nonagenarian (not nono-)

nonconformist but note *the Nonconformist Church* and *Nonconformist churches* (buildings); see **Churches** special section (page 172)

non-cooperation see **co-operate**

none almost always takes the singular verb, eg, "none is available at present". But occasionally a plural is permissible, eg, "None are better singers than the Welsh" or "none of them have done their best" (where the inelegant alternative would be "none of them has done his or her best"). See **neither**

nonetheless one word

non-existent

non-profitmaking

noon (not 12 noon, 12am or 12pm). See **midnight**

normalcy avoid; use *normality* instead

north, northeast, northern for when to cap, see **compass points**

Northern Ireland see **Ireland**

Northumberland (county); Northumbria is a health, police or tourist authority

North York Moors (not North Yorkshire Moors); see **Yorkshire**

notable (no middle *e*)

Note cap in the diplomatic sense

not only ... followed by *but* (and usually) *also*; often better to say simply *both ... and*

nuclear terms should be used with precision. Take special care not to confuse *fission* and *fusion*

numbers write from one to ten in full, 11 upwards as numerals except when they are approximations, eg, "about thirty people turned up". Keep consistency within a sentence: write "the number injured rose from eight to fourteen", and do not mix fractions and decimals. At the start of a sentence, write all numbers in full.
  ordinals: write out up to hundredth, then 101st, 122nd etc, except with names such as 42nd Street, 38th parallel etc. See **birthday, millions, currencies, fractions**

numberplate (on vehicles etc); one word; see **motoring terms**

Nuremberg (not -burg)

Nursing, Royal College of (not Nurses)

NVQ national vocational qualification; note l/c when spelt out

O...

oblivious of means *forgetful of*, *unaware of*. It does not mean ignorant or uncomprehending

O'Brien, Conor Cruise, likewise **Edna**

obscenities "four-letter words" and profanities should be avoided. However, in direct quotes and where they are essential to the story, style obscenities with asterisks: f***, c*** etc

occupied territories, the all l/c

occurred (not occured)

o'clock see **times**

octogenarian

octopuses plural of octopus (not octopi)

Oder-Neisse Line (boundary between Poland and Germany)

Odone, Cristina (not Christina), journalist

OECD Organisation for Economic Co-operation and Development

of avoid expressions such as "all of the people attending", "half of the children replied"; say simply "all the people", "half the children" etc

of all time do not use this phrase, as in "best golfer of all time", in any circumstances

offbeat no hyphen

Office for National Statistics (no longer the Central Statistical Office)

Office for Standards in Education, but *Ofsted* usually sufficient on its own. See **regulators**

officers (naval and military); do not describe ratings or NCOs as *officers*, especially in headlines and captions. See **Armed Forces** special section (page 164)

oil-drilling, oil-fired, oil-slick, oil-tanker but note *oildrum, oilfield, oilrig* and *oil platform*. See **Brent Spar**

OK rather than *okay*

Old Etonian, Old Harrovian etc

Old Masters caps to avoid confusion

Olivier, Laurence (not Lawrence), the late Lord Olivier

Olympics can be used as a short form of *the Olympic Games*. Similarly, *the Games* (always capped) can be used. Always cap Olympics and Olympic even when used adjectivally, eg, *an Olympic athlete*. Note *International Olympic Committee* (no final *s* on Olympic)

ombudsman, ombudswoman keep l/c in general context, eg, "he referred the matter to the ombudsman"; but cap for specifics, as in *the Banking Ombudsman*, *the Legal Services Ombudsman*, and even the unofficial title of *Parliamentary Ombudsman* (the Parliamentary Commissioner for Administration). Do not confuse the Parliamentary Ombudsman with the Parliamentary Commissioner for Standards, an entirely separate post

on behalf of frequently misused phrase. It means *in the interest of* (a person etc) or *as representative of* (eg, "acting on behalf of his client" is correct). It must not be used as a verbose way of saying *by*; eg, "the book betrays a lack of understanding on behalf of the author" is wrong

ONdigital

one use the singular verb in structures such as "one in three says that . . ." See **nearly**. In first-person pieces, try to avoid the use of *one* as a synonym of *I*

One Nation Tories, One Nation politicians etc note cap *O* and cap *N*

one-time do not use as synonym of *former* as in "one-time chairman" etc

One 2 One; the mobile phone company (note spaces)

ongoing avoid this ugly adjective; use *continuing* if necessary

online one word in computer context

only take great care to place *only* before the word or phrase it qualifies; "she *only* touched the key, but did not press it; she touched *only* the key, not the switch; she touched the *only* key". Similarly, "he only played cricket" is wrong; "he played only cricket" is correct

on to unlike *into,* two words usually better than one, as in "she moved on to better things", though "he collapsed onto the floor" is acceptable. As a general rule, use *onto* as little as possible

Opec the Organisation of Petroleum Exporting Countries

opencast mining

open-heart surgery note also *open-door policy* (if this overworked phrase has to be used); *open-plan living room*

operations see medical terms

ophthalmologist, ophthalmic etc (not opthalmic)

Opposition the same cap or l/c rules apply as to Government – cap as a noun but generally l/c as adjective; eg, "He accused the Opposition of lying", but "He said it was an opposition lie". See **Politics** special section (page 181)

or need not be preceded by *either,* though it is strengthened thereby if two options are mentioned. Usually avoid a comma before it

oral do not confuse with *verbal*; *oral* means pertaining to the mouth, often in the spoken context (eg, *the oral tradition, by word of mouth*); *verbal* means pertaining to words (contrasted with, eg, physical or choral). See **verbal**

Orders in Council are *approved*, not signed, by the Queen

ordinals see **numbers**

Ordnance Survey note *ordnance* in military contexts; but *ordinance* as in regulations

Orient, the wherever possible, use *the East*. The adjective is l/c *oriental*. The East London football club is *Leyton Orient*

orientate, orientation prefer to *orient, oriented* etc. See **disorientate**

Orkney, or **the Orkney Islands** (not the Orkneys); see **Shetland**

Oscar Award(s), or **the Oscars** registered trademarks, so cap

OSCE the Organisation for Security and Co-operation in Europe, has replaced the former CSCE (Conference on Security and Co-operation in Europe)

Ouija board proprietary term, so cap

Outback, the (Australia)

outdoor adjective; but note *the outdoors*

outpatients, inpatients no hyphen

OutRage! (homosexual "outing" group)

outside (never *outside of*)

-out suffixes in nouns, generally join up rather than hyphenate, as in *fallout, knockout, printout, callout, dropout, bailout* etc; but note *to fall out* etc

Outward Bound must be used only when specifically referring to the work or courses of the Outward Bound Trust Ltd, and never in general use in phrases such as *outward bound-style activities*. Use alternatives such as *outdoor pursuits, adventure training, outdoor adventure courses* etc. Outward Bound's lawyers pounce on every perceived infringement of its service mark. Take care

over do not use as a synonym of *more than* when followed by a number, eg, "she waited over four hours for the train" should be ". . . more than four hours . . ."; "there were over 60 victims" should be ". . . more than 60 . . .". See **more than**

over as prefix wherever the word does not look too ugly, dispense with the hyphen, even when this leads to a double *r* in the middle: *overcapacity, overestimate, overreact, override, overrule, overuse, overvalue*; an obvious exception where the hyphen is essential is *over-age*

overall one word as adjective, but use sparingly

overly do not use as an alternative for *over* or *too*

Overseas Development Administration (not Agency)

owing to see **due to**

Oxbridge be sparing in using the term as a "catch-all" for Oxford and Cambridge Universities

Oxford University colleges and halls are:
All Souls College; Balliol College; Blackfriars; Brasenose College; Campion Hall; Christ Church; Corpus Christi College; Exeter College; Green College; Greyfriars; Harris Manchester College; Hertford College; Jesus College; Keble College; Kellogg College; Lady Margaret Hall; Linacre College; Lincoln College; Magdalen College; Mansfield College; Merton College; New College; Nuffield College; Oriel College; Pembroke College; The Queen's College; Regent's Park College; St Anne's College; St Antony's College; St Benet's Hall; St Catherine's College; St Cross College; St Edmund Hall; St Hilda's College; St Hugh's College; St John's College; St Peter's College; Somerville College; Templeton College; Trinity College; University College; Wadham College; Wolfson College; Worcester College

P...

p's and q's see **apostrophes**

Pacific Rim, South Pacific, North Pacific etc

page 1, page 3, page 189 etc but note *a Page 3 Girl*

paintings titles in italic. See **Arts** special section (page 169)

Pakistani use both for the people of Pakistan and adjectivally, eg, *Pakistani culture*

palace cap in full names, such as Blenheim Palace, thereafter *the palace*. However, note that *the Palace* is acceptable for Buckingham Palace in stories about royalty. See **Royal Family**

Palace of Holyroodhouse, Edinburgh

palaeo- (not paleo-); similarly *palaeography* etc

Palestinian National Authority (not Palestine) – usually *the Palestinian Authority* will suffice; but note *the Palestine Liberation Organisation* (PLO)

Palmer-Tomkinson, Tara and **Santa**

paparazzi

paperboy, papergirl

paraffin see **kerosene**

paraphernalia (not paraphanalia)

paratroops general term for troops dropped by parachute; a *parachutist* is a specialist in the activity. Note *The Parachute Regiment*

Pardo Palace (royal palace on the outskirts of Madrid); the Madrid art gallery is the *Prado*

Parent's Charter

Paris some of the more familiar place names prone to error are the *Champs Elysées*, the *Elysée Palace*, the *Quai d'Orsay*, the *Jardin du Luxembourg* (not de), the *Jardin des Tuileries* (not de) and the *Jeu de Paume* (not Pomme)

Parker Bowles, Camilla no hyphen

Parkinson's disease

Parliament cap always in British context, and in overseas contexts when the word forms part of the institution, eg, the European Parliament, Canadian Parliament. However, note l/c for the Spanish parliament (the Cortes), the Russian parliament (Duma), the Israeli parliament (Knesset), Polish parliament (Sejm) etc; and l/c when it is only a mooted body, such as the English parliament.

Also, l/c *parliamentary*, even in *parliamentary private secretary* (abbreviated to PPS) because there are many of them; but note *Parliamentary Labour Party* (PLP), of which there is one, and similarly *Parliamentary Ombudsman*. See **PLP**, **ombudsman**, and **Politics** special section (page 181)

Parliamentary Commissioner for Standards caps for the new post created in the light of the Neill (formerly Nolan) Committee on Standards in Public Life. He must not be referred to as the *Parliamentary Ombudsman*, who is the *Parliamentary Commissioner for Administration*. See **ombudsman**

partially, partly *partially* is of *degree*, eg, *partially deaf*; *partly* is of *extension*, eg, *partly under water*

participles beware the grammar trap of the disconnected (or unrelated) participle; eg, "Judging by the lingering camera shots, X's luck was not about to change" is wrong – the present participle *judging* has to have a following noun or pronoun in agreement (in other words, X's luck is not doing the judging). So the sentence has to be rephrased, as "Judging by the lingering camera shots, I saw that X's luck . . .", or "To judge from the lingering camera shots, X's luck . . ."

parties (political) cap *Labour Party*, *Conservative Party*, or any other party; also overseas parties, such as *Republican Party*, *Democratic Party* (though usually *Republicans* and *Democrats* will suffice). See **Tory**, **Politics** special section (page 181)

part-time, part-timer note hyphens

partygoer see **-goer**

Passchendaele

passer-by, passers-by

past use rather than *last* in such phrases as "the past two weeks". See **last**

pastime

past tense (of verbs); almost always prefer the shorter form using final *-t* where appropriate; eg, *spelt* (not spelled), *dreamt* (not dreamed); but never earnt for *earned*

Patient's Charter

PAYE pay as you earn; note caps

Paymaster General

payout, payoff no hyphens

Peace Implementation Council (in the former Yugoslavia, part of the Dayton agreement)

peacekeeping, peacemaking etc no hyphens

peal (of bells); but **peel** (of an orange etc)

Pearl Harbor (not Harbour)

pedal (as in bicycle); note *peddle* (as in selling drugs or advocating ideas). A *pedaller* is someone who pedals a bike; a *pedlar* is a small trader; and a drug-pusher is a *peddler*

peers a peer or a peeress has a seat in the House of Lords. A female life peer is a peeress usually referred to as Baroness X. After the first mention of the Marquess of Paddington, Earl of Euston, Viscount Pimlico or Lord Holborn, call them all Lord Paddington, Lord Euston etc. See **Titles** special section (page 189)

pejorative (not perjorative)

Peking use only in phrases such as *Peking duck* or *Peking man*. The city is now *Beijing*. Note *pekinese dogs*. See **Chinese names**

Peloponnese

PEN (international association of writers)

peninsula never *peninsular* when used as a noun; peninsular is the adjective, as in the Peninsular War

pensioners take care with this word. Some readers take exception to "ambiguous" usage, so it should strictly be confined to people drawing their state pension (men at 65, women at 60). If in doubt, write *the elderly*, or as last resort, *senior citizen*. See **elderly**

pension funds (not pensions funds as plural)

people use rather than *persons* wherever appropriate; exceptions would be "the law is no respecter of persons" or the ubiquitous *missing persons*. Take care with the apostrophe: remember that people is a plural, so the normal use is apostrophe *s*, eg, "it is the people's wish"; very occasionally, *peoples* in the sense of *races* can take an *s* apostrophe, eg, "the African peoples' common heritage"

Pep(s) personal equity plan; spell out in general news, but not necessarily in Business stories

Pepsi-Cola hyphen; similarly *Coca-Cola*

per try to avoid in phrases such as "six times per year"; "six times a year" is better

per cent always takes figures rather than the word, eg, 3 per cent, not three per cent. Usually use decimals rather than fractions (3.25 per cent rather than 31/4 per cent). Use % sign in headlines, never pc, and spell out *per cent* in text

percentage, proportion do not use as a synonym of *part* or *many* if that is all they mean in a sentence: eg, instead of "a large percentage of parents objected" write "many parents objected"

percentage points take care. If the mortgage rate rises from 8 per cent to 10 per cent, it does not rise by 2 per cent, but by two percentage points. Similarly if a political party's support drops from 50 per cent to 40 per cent in an opinion poll, it has lost ten percentage points or 20 per cent of its support

perestroika not italics

performance-related pay

Performing Right Society (not Rights)

Pergau dam (Malaysia)

Persia use Iran for the modern state, and never Persian Gulf except in historical context. See **Gulf**

Personal Investment Authority (not Investments); abbreviate to PIA

personnel prefer *people* or *employees* or *workers* wherever possible

Perspex trade name, so cap

peseta do not abbreviate the Spanish currency in any context

Peterhouse (Cambridge college); never takes College after the name. Neither does Christ Church, Oxford; nor do any Oxford or Cambridge colleges ending with Hall, eg, Lady Margaret Hall. See **Cambridge University, Oxford University**

petfood no hyphen; similarly *catfood*, *dogfood*

phalangist (Lebanon); see **falangist**

Pharaoh (not -oah); note l/c adjective *pharaonic*

phenomenon plural *phenomena*; beware the use of *phenomenal* as a cliché meaning remarkable or big

Philips (Dutch electronics company); note no apostrophe for *Phillips* (auction house)

phone now so common that it is permissible in text as well as headlines

phoney (not phony)

phosphorus noun; but note *phosphorous*, *phosphoric* (adjectives); *phosphorescence*

photo call two words; similarly *photo opportunity*

photo-finish

photofit l/c; but note cap for *Identikit*

pidgin English (not pigeon)

piecemeal, piecework

pigeonholed

pigheaded

Pigott-Smith, Tim (not Piggott), actor, but **Lester Piggott**, jockey

pilgrims l/c; but note *the Pilgrim Fathers*; note also John Bunyan's *The Pilgrim's Progress*

Pill, the (contraceptive)

Pimm's (the drink)

PIN personal identification number (not Pin); note that *PIN number* is a tautology

pinstripes (-d)

pitbull (terrier)

pitstop (motor racing)

PKK, the Kurdish Workers' Party (not Kurdistan...)

place names refer to the *Bartholomew Gazetteer* for place names in England, Wales and Scotland, and *The Times Atlas of the World* for the rest of the world. But there are exceptions: beware the new Welsh county names, and see **unitary authorities, foreign places, Spanish regions**

place name constructions two ugly devices to avoid are, eg, a *Gosport, Hampshire, housewife,* and *Manchester's Piccadilly station;* say instead a *housewife from Gosport, Hampshire,* and *Piccadilly station, Manchester*

Plaid Cymru (Welsh Nationalist Party)

plane as in *on a higher plane* (not plain)

planes try to avoid in text as a synonym of aircraft, and be very sparing in headlines, where *jets* (where applicable) or *aircraft* are always better. See **aircraft**

play-off

plays titles in italics. See **Arts** special section (page 169)

PlayStation

plc all l/c; can usually be dropped from company names; see **Ltd**

PLP Parliamentary Labour Party; see **Politics** special section (page 181)

plurals make corporate bodies and institutions singular unless this looks odd. Thus "The National Trust is . . .", but sports teams are plural, eg, "Arsenal were worth their 8-0 lead". Whether singular or plural, always maintain consistency within a story

plus, minus do not use as variants of *and* or *without*

point-to-point

poetess avoid, use *poet* instead; see **feminine designations**

Poet Laureate caps; note plural *Poets Laureate*

Polaroid trade name, so cap

Polgar, Judit see **chess names**

police forces cap the word Police when it is part of the full name of the force. This applies to the following forces: *Metropolitan Police, City of London Police, British Transport Police, Ministry of Defence Police, Bedfordshire Police, Dorset Police* (Force), *Essex Police, Greater Manchester Police, Humberside Police, Lincolnshire Police, Merseyside Police, Northamptonshire Police, Northumbria Police, North Yorkshire Police, South Yorkshire Police, Staffordshire Police, Surrey Police, Sussex Police, Thames Valley Police, West Midlands Police, West Yorkshire Police, Dyfed-Powys Police, North Wales Police, Central Scotland Police, Grampian Police, Lothian and Borders*

Police, Strathclyde Police, Tayside Police

Other forces use Constabulary instead of Police (eg, *Cleveland Constabulary, Kent Constabulary*), so either give that full title or, more commonly, write *Cleveland police, Kent police* etc. Do not cap when referring to a local division, eg, *Luton police*, or *police in Luton*. If in doubt, consult *Whitaker's Almanack* under "Police Authorities"

policemen take care with this word. Certain senior officers, men and women, regularly chide us for using *policemen* when we mean *police officers*. If in doubt, use the latter.

police ranks wherever possible outside lists, avoid the inelegant abbreviated forms such as *Det Con, Det Chief Insp*. Spell out, even if inconvenient sometimes. An exception is *PC*, or *WPC* (for Woman Police Constable). *PC* also acceptable in headlines. Compound titles do not take hyphens in the police force. Detective Sergeant X becomes Sergeant X after the first mention. Inspector and all ranks above are usually Mr after the first mention. See **Chief Constable**

Police Staff College at Bramshill, Hampshire; or simply *the police college* (l/c), Bramshill

policyholder, policymaker but note *policy document*

Politburo usually cap

Pope, the not usually necessary to give his full name, eg, Pope John Paul II (unless several Popes are mentioned in a story), but always cap. Note *papacy, pontiff* (l/c). See **Churches** special section (page 172)

poppadum

populist should not be confused with, or used as a synonym of, *popular*; it means supporting the interest of ordinary people, or pandering to mass public taste

Porritt, Jonathon despite his baronetcy, prefers not to use Sir

Portakabin trade name, so cap

possibly like most qualifiers, this word can (usually) be omitted

postal addresses in news and features, prefer to say *Bromley, southeast London* (rather than Kent), and *Kingston upon Thames, southwest London* (rather than Surrey) etc. This leaves the old counties such as Middlesex to be used only in their historical or sporting contexts.

Also avoid the clumsy possessive form such as *Manchester's Moss Side, London's East End*; say *Moss Side, Manchester, the East End of London*. There is no need to use postcodes except when giving an address for information. See **addresses**

postcode (no hyphen)

postgraduate, undergraduate noun and adjective both one word

Post-Modern caps, hyphen; see **artistic movements**

post mortem wherever possible write *post-mortem examination* in reports, though *post mortem* is acceptable nowadays in headlines

Post Office caps for the corporation, but l/c *post office* for the branches. Note also *sub-post office, sub-postmaster, Post Office Counters, Royal Mail, ParcelForce*

postwar, prewar adjectives, commonly referring to Second World War. Do not use adverbially (as in "there were a million jobless prewar")

potatoes plural; similarly *tomatoes*

pothole (as in caving or road surfaces); similarly *potholer*

PoW (prisoner of war); note plural *PoWs*

PowerGen

PPE the university degree is philosophy, politics and economics (not politics, philosophy etc)

practical, practicable do not confuse. *Practical* means adapted to actual conditions or (of a person) able to make things function well; *practicable* means capable of being effected or accomplished

practice noun; but **practise** (verb). It is an inexcusable *practice* for sub-editors to confuse the two; writers should *practise* getting it right

Prado gallery, Madrid see **Pardo**

praesidium (not presidium)

praying mantis (not preying)

prearrange

predilection (not predeliction)

pre-empt

Premier do not use in text as a synonym of *Prime Minister*, though very occasionally its use in the headline of a foreign story (never British) may be permitted. Generally, confine the word to heads of government of the Canadian provinces or Australian states, when it should take a cap. *Premiership* is preferable to *prime-ministership*

premiere (of a play, ballet etc); no accent

Premiership (football); refer to the *FA Carling Premiership* at first mention, *the Premiership* thereafter, for the top division in English football; the organisation that runs it is the *FA Premier League*.

Similarly, the lower divisions form the *Nationwide* (no longer Endsleigh) *League, first division, second division* (note l/c) etc; this competition is run by the *Football League*. See **Sports** special section (page 185)

premise (assumption in an argument); note the word *premises* (property) takes the plural verb, eg, "the premises are well positioned"

Premium Bonds caps

prepositional verbs avoid wherever possible. Examples such as *measure up to, get on with* are acceptable on the odd occasion. Others such as *consult with, meet with* (where the preposition is tautologous) must never be used

Pre-Raphaelite

Presbyterian beware, especially with the adjective *Scots*. See **Church, Churches** special section (page 172)

present better than *current* but often redundant

President cap *the President* of any country, also *President of the European Commission* at first and all subsequent mentions; but l/c *presidency* (as in *the French presidency of the EU*). Also note that *presidents of companies* or *organisations* normally take l/c, though this rule should be relaxed for leading national organisations, such as *President of the Law Society* and *President of the TUC*

press always l/c except in titles such as *the Press Complaints Commission*. See **broadsheet**

prestigious try to avoid this much-overworked word and find an appropriate substitute such as *highly regarded, admired, eminent, esteemed, leading, noted, outstanding, powerful* etc

pretension but note *pretentious*

prevaricate (to speak or act evasively); do not confuse with **procrastinate** (to defer action, to be dilatory)

preventive (not preventative)

PricewaterhouseCoopers (*PwC* for short), the merged accountants

prime meridian l/c

Prime Minister cap for every country. But l/c when referring to an unspecific, eg, "he would make a good prime minister". Never say, eg, Prime Minister Tony Blair or even Tony Blair, the Prime Minister; write instead *Tony Blair* at first mention, then *the Prime Minister* at next mention. Never use Premier for the British Prime Minister, and never use PM even in headlines. See **Premier**

primeval

Prince avoid the familiar forms of Prince Charles and Prince Philip at least until they have been given their full designation of *Prince of Wales* and *Duke of Edinburgh*; even then, prefer *the Prince* and *the Duke* at subsequent mentions. Note *The Prince's Trust*. See **royal, Royal Family**

Princess of Wales see **Diana, Princess of Wales**

Princes Street, Edinburgh

principal noun or adjective; means chief, main, important, head etc; eg, *the principal of a college,* or *the team's principal objective.* Do not confuse with **principle**, which is a noun meaning concept, ideal, rule, moral etc; eg, *her Christian principles*

Principality, the cap in Welsh context

printout

prior to avoid wherever possible; use *before*

Prison Service note caps and *s* in *Prisons Board*; also caps for *Director-General of the Prison Service* and *Chief Inspector of Prisons*; see **Governor, Probation Service**

prison visitors be careful to differentiate clearly between two groups of prison visitors:
a. members of the National Association of Prison Visitors, who visit prisoners in the "social" sense of visiting
b. members of prison boards of visitors, who visit as watchdogs in an official role and sometimes make recommendations on matters such as discipline and security

Private Finance Initiative (PFI), sometimes now known as *Public Private Partnerships* (initial caps)

private sector, public sector do not use hyphens even when employed adjectivally, eg, *public sector pay* (as *high street shopping*)

privatised industries see **regulators**

Privileges, Committee of

Privy Council but note *Privy Counsellors* (not Councillors)

prizewinner one word

Probation Service caps; similarly *Prison Service*

probe use only in a scientific, medical or space context. Never to be used as *inquiry,* even in headlines

problem be sparing with this overworked word

procrastinate (to defer action, to be dilatory). See **prevaricate**

Procter & Gamble note *-er* and ampersand

Procurator Fiscal (Crown prosecutor in Scotland); see **Courts** special section (page 176)

profanities see **obscenities**

Professor caps for *Professor of History* etc; thereafter *the professor* or *Professor X*; see **university posts**

proffer, proffered (not profer, preferred)

profits especially in Business stories, should always state the basis of the figure (pre-tax, operating etc)

program (computers); *programme* (the arts etc)

pro-life beware this contentious phrase for the anti-abortion lobby (especially in US context); use the phrase *anti-abortion* wherever possible, but when "pro-life" is unavoidable always quote it

Proms acceptable abbreviation of Promenade Concerts; note also *Promenaders* and *the Last Night of the Proms*

prone (lying face-down); note *supine* (face-up)

propeller (not -or)

prophecy noun; note verb **prophesy**

proportion see **percentage**

pros and cons

protagonist means a *supporter* (of either side) in a debate or quarrel; it does not mean *advocate* or *proponent*

protégé

protester (never -or); but see **demonstrator**

Protestant beware of using for all Christians who are not Roman Catholic. See **Churches** special section (page 172)

proven *not proven* is the Scottish legal verdict. In general use, prefer *proved* to *proven*; but *proven* and *unproven* may be used as a colloquial alternative

provided that (not *providing that*)

Province, the see **Ireland**

provinces, provincial take great care of these words in the context of "outside London". Many regard them as patronising; use *the regions* or *regional* wherever possible

prurient means having an unhealthy obsession with sex; it does not mean puritanical

PSBR public sector borrowing requirement

public house *pub* is now fully acceptable in text or headlines

public interest immunity certificate abbreviate to PIIC, or simply *the certificate*

publicly (never publically)

Public Record Office (not Records)

public school independent school is now a preferable term; use *public schoolboys*, *public schoolgirls*, if necessary

public sector see **private sector**

Pulitzer prizes see **Nobel prize** for when to cap

pullout noun, one word; but note *to pull out*

punctuation some important reminders:
a. Commas keep commas inside quotes in the following type of "broken" sentence: "The trouble is," he said, "that this is a contentious issue." Omit the comma before *if, unless, before, since, when* unless the rhythm or sense of the sentence demands it. Avoid the so-called *Oxford comma*; say "he ate bread, butter and jam" rather than "he ate bread, butter, and jam".
b. Dashes do not use in place of commas. Too many dashes can be ugly and disruptive.
c. Punctuation marks place inside inverted commas if they relate to the words quoted, outside if they relate to the main sentence, eg, She is going to classes in "health and beauty". If the whole sentence is a quotation, the final point goes inside, eg, "Beauty is truth, truth beauty."

d. Interrogation marks never use with indirect questions or rhetorical questions, eg, "She asked why he did not laugh."

e. Parentheses use sparingly; try to use commas instead.

f. Conjunctions *And* and *but* may occasionally be used at the beginning of a sentence, especially for emphasis.

g. Ellipses use three points with full space after last word, then thin spacing between points, then full space before next word, eg, *not only . . . but also*

puns an enjoyable device for headline writers. Restrict their use to funny or light stories or features and if in doubt, avoid; but if irresistible, make sure they are in good taste

Puritan (16th/17th-century religious group); do not use as a contemporary adjective; *puritanical* is just permitted

putsch (military seizure of power, as in coup)

pygmy, pygmies

Pyramids the three main Pyramids at Giza (including the Great Pyramid) should be capped. But there are many other pyramids (l/c) throughout Egypt

pyrrhic l/c, as in *pyrrhic victory*

Q . . .

Qantas (not Quantas)

qat (hypnotic drug); preferable to *kat* or *khat*

QC, MP place commas each side when used after name

QCA Qualifications and Curriculum Authority; spell out at first mention. It is an amalgamation (from autumn 1997) of the *National Council for Vocational Qualifications* and the *School Curriculum and Assessment Authority*

QE2 normally spell out *Queen Elizabeth 2* at first mention, thereafter *QE2* or simply *the ship*

Qom, Iran (not Qum)

quadriplegia, quadriplegic (not quadra-)

quality press prefer *broadsheet*. See **broadsheet**

quango short for quasi-autonomous non-governmental organisation; no need to spell out or to quote

quantum leap avoid this cliché wherever possible

quarter sessions like assizes, no longer function, having been replaced by Crown Courts

Quebeckers rather than *Quebecois*

Queen, the aim at keeping *the* in headlines. Note caps for *the Queen's Speech* (to Parliament) and *the Queen's Birthday Honours*. See **Royal Family, New Year Honours**

Queen Elizabeth the Queen Mother no commas; always this style at first mention, thereafter *the Queen Mother*

Queen Elizabeth II Conference Centre, London (not QE2 or any other variant)

Queens, New York

Queensberry, Marquess of also *Queensberry Rules*

Queen's Club

Queens' College, Cambridge but note **The Queen's College, Oxford** (see **Cambridge University** and **Oxford University**); also note *The Queen's University of Belfast,* usually shortened to *Queen's University, Belfast* or simply *Queen's, Belfast*

Queens Park Rangers thereafter QPR

queueing note middle *e*

questionnaire

Question Time, Prime Minister's Questions caps, but note l/c *questions* to the Prime Minister, Foreign Secretary etc. See **Politics** special section (page 181)

quicker never use as an adverb – always use *more quickly*. Confine *quicker* to adjectival comparison, eg, "he started at a quicker pace"

quid pro quo not italic

quiz show no hyphen; similarly *chat show, game show, talk show* etc

quotation marks (inverted commas); remember, single quotes in headlines, straps and display panels; double quotes in captions and key-decks. The only other use for single inverted commas is quotations within quotations.

Avoid inverted commas in sentences where they are clearly unnecessary, eg, *He described the attack as "outrageous"*.

Quotation marks are no longer to be used for works of art.

See **inverted commas, italics**

See also **punctuation** (paragraph c) for when punctuation goes inside or outside quotation marks

quotes direct quotes should be corrected only to remove the solecisms and other errors that occur in speech but look silly in print. Always take care that quotes are correctly attributed; and especially that literary or biblical quotations are 100 per cent accurate

R...

race references to race should be used only when relevant to the sense of the story. The word is often better replaced by *people, nation, group* etc

racecourse, racehorse, racetrack see **horse**, and **Sports** special section (page 185)

racked as in *racked by doubts, pain* etc; (not *wracked*)

racket (for tennis; not *racquet*); the game is *rackets*

RADA the Royal Academy of Dramatic Art; all caps

radio compounds are hyphenated in the wireless context (eg, *radio-telephone*); but one word when they concern rays (eg, *radioactive, radioisotope, radiotherapy*). Broadcasting frequencies are measured in *megahertz* (MHz) and *kilohertz* (kHz)

radio ham this term should strictly be applied only to licensed amateur radio operators, who are offended when it is used to apply to unlicensed "eavesdroppers" spying on private phone calls etc. Take care

Radio 1, 2, 3, 4, Radio 5 Live note also *Classic FM, BBC Radio*. But with foreign stations, usually l/c, eg, *Israel radio, Haiti radio, Moscow radio* etc; cap only if it is the specific name of the station or organisation

RAF Regiment (Corps within the Royal Air Force)

rail franchise director l/c; informal and acceptable short form of the

Director of Passenger Rail Franchising (caps). The *Rail Regulator* takes caps; see **regulators**

rainforest one word

raison d'être use italics

Raleigh, Sir Walter (not Ralegh)

R&B abbreviation for rhythm and blues

ranging from overworked and often unnecessary phrase. There must be a scale in which the elements might be ranged: "ranging from 15 to 25 years" is correct, "a crowd ranging from priests to golfers" is not

ranks see **police ranks, Armed Forces** special section (page 164)

Ranks Hovis McDougall but note *(The) Rank Organisation*

Rapid Reaction Force caps

rarefied, rarefy (not *rarified*)

rateable

rave acceptable in context as a musical event; see **gig**

razzmatazz

re- whenever possible, run the prefix on to the word it qualifies, eg, *readmission, remake, reorganise, rework,* etc; but there are two main classes of exceptions:
a. where the word after re- begins with *e*, eg, *re-election, re-emerge, re-examine, re-enter* etc;
b. where there could be serious ambiguity in compounds such as *re-creation (recreation), re-cover (recover), re-dress (redress).* See **hyphens**

realpolitik not italic

rebut means to argue to the contrary, producing evidence; *to refute* is to win such an argument. Neither should be used as a synonym of *reject* or *deny*. Nor should they be used for *dispute* or *respond to*

receive "receiving an injury" is to be discouraged, though not banned. Prefer to say *sustained* or *suffered;* and never say someone received a broken leg etc – prefer *suffered a broken leg* or, better still, *broke a leg.* See **injure**

reckless (not wreckless); synonym for rash or foolhardy

record never write "set a new record", "was an all-time record" etc, where both the qualifiers are tautologous

recorders for when to cap, see **Courts** special section (page 176)

recrudescence do not confuse with *resurgence* or *revival*. It means *worsening*, in the sense of reopening wounds or recurring diseases

redbrick (university); but note a *red-brick* building

Red Planet (informal name for Mars); caps

referendum plural *referendums*, as with *conundrums, stadiums, forums* and most words ending in *-um*. But note *millennia, strata*

refute take care with this word. See **rebut**

Regent's Park

regimen should be restricted to medical contexts – a prescribed course of exercise, way of life, diet etc. Do not use as a synonym of *regime* (government or administrative contexts)

register office (not registry office)

Register of Members' Interests caps; see **Politics** special section (page 181)

Registrar (Oxford); but note *Registrary* (Cambridge)

Registrar-General

regulators of the privatised industries and the consumer watchdog should be styled as follows:
Director-General of Electricity and Gas Supply, who heads Office of Gas Supply (Ofgas) and can be shortened to the *gas regulator*, and who also heads Office of Electricity Regulation (Offer) and can be shortened to the *electricity regulator*
Director-General of Water Services (heads Office of Water Services, Ofwat), or the *water regulator*
Director-General of Telecommunications (heads Office of Telecommunications, Oftel), or the *telecommunications regulator*
Rail Regulator (Office of the Rail Regulator) – cap as it is the official title; note that the *Office of Passenger Rail Franchising* (Opraf) is separate
Director-General of Fair Trading (Office of Fair Trading, OFT) best not to abbreviate – use *consumer watchdog* as alternative

Reith Lecture(s)

reject see **rebut**

relatively see **comparatively**

Religious Right (in American politics); caps. See **Right**

remainder avoid as a synonym of *the rest*

REME the Royal Electrical and Mechanical Engineers (never Reme). See **Armed Forces** special section (page 164)

Remembrance Sunday prefer to Day

Renaissance, the but l/c *renaissance* as synonym of *revival* or *rebirth*

repellent (noun or adjective), not repellant

report l/c in titles of official documents such as *Taylor report*

reportedly avoid this slack word, which suggests that the material's source is not clear

Republic of Ireland, or **Irish Republic** see **Ireland**

republican l/c except when in an official name, such as *the Republican Party* or *Republicans* (US). See **Ireland**

rerun

Resolution cap in context of UN, eg, *Resolution 688*

respect of avoid "in respect of" whenever possible; never write "in respect to"

responsible people bear responsibility, things do not. Storms are not responsible for damage; they cause it. Avoid the phrase "the IRA *claimed responsibility for* the bombing"; say instead "the IRA *admitted causing* the bombing"

restaurateur (never restauranteur)

result in avoid this lazy phrase and always find an alternative, such as *cause, bring, create, evoke, lead to* etc

re-use one of the *re-* words where the hyphen is essential

Reuters use this form now in every context (no longer Reuter)

Reveille like Last Post, is *sounded,* not played

Revelation, Book of (not Revelations)

reverend at first mention, the style is *the Rev Tom Jones,* then *Mr Jones.* Never write "the Rev Jones" or (even worse) "Rev Jones" (which is as great a solecism as calling Sir Norman Fowler "Sir

Fowler"). A parson and his wife are referred to as *the Rev Tom and Mrs Jones*. See **archbishops, Churches** special section (page 172)

Review caps in names of government programmes such as *Strategic Defence Review, Comprehensive Spending Review*

Reykjavik, Iceland

rhinoceroses (plural)

Rhys-Jones, Sophie now the *Countess of Wessex* (subsequent mentions the *Countess*). See **Titles** special section (page 189)

RIBA abbreviation of the Royal Institute of British Architects; all caps

Richter scale measures the energy released by an earthquake. It runs from 0 to 8; write "the earthquake measured 6 on the Richter scale"

RICS Royal Institution of Chartered Surveyors (not Institute); note caps

riffle, riffling as in flicking through papers or clothes on a rail; note *rifling* in the sense of ransacking

Right, the cap in the political context when referring to a group of like-minded individuals, eg, "The Right added to John Major's dilemma on the EU"; but l/c in "the party swung to the right". When the Right is qualified, generally keep the adjective l/c, eg, *the far Right* (but note *the Religious Right* in the US). Also, *the right wing, right-wing contenders, rightwingers*. See **Left**

rigmarole (not rigamarole)

ring-fence hyphen

Rio Tinto (no longer Rio Tinto-Zinc or RTZ)

riverbank one word

rivers cap in context of *River Thames, Mississippi River* (or simply *the Thames, the Mississippi* etc). Similarly, cap *estuary* when part of the name. See **Thames**

riveting try to avoid its clichéd use as a metaphor

roadblock, roadbuilding, roadbuilder etc

road rage wherever possible, quote at first mention (ie, "road rage"); but not thereafter, nor in headlines

roads as tautologous to write "the M5 motorway" as "the A435 road", but correct to say "the M40 London to Birmingham motorway".

Unnecessary to define the M25 as London's orbital motorway, but generally, define a road geographically unless context is clear

Robert the Bruce prefer to Robert Bruce; subsequent mentions *the Bruce*

rock'n'roll

Rollerblade proprietary term, so cap. The American company's lawyers insist that even Rollerblading is capped; use *in-line skates/skating* instead

rollerskate, rollercoaster

roll-on, roll-off (as in ferries); abbreviate to *ro-ro*

rollover (as in National Lottery); no hyphen

Rolls-Royce

Roman Catholic see **Catholic**

Romania (not Rumania); see **Ceausescu**

Roman numerals usually no full points, eg, *Edward VIII, Article XVI, Part II, Psalm xxiii*. But in official documents, to designate sub-sections, use the points, eg, *i., ii., iv.,* etc

roofs (not rooves)

rooms use *dining room, living room, drawing room, laundry room* (no hyphens except when adjectival, eg, *living-room carpet*); but note *bathroom, bedroom*

rottweiler l/c; see dogs

row be sparing in the use of this word, especially in headlines. Alternatives are *rift, split, clash* etc, and *dispute* in text. However, *row* is not banned

Rowntree be sure to distinguish between the *Joseph Rowntree Foundation*, a charity and independent funder of social policy research and development; and the *Joseph Rowntree Reform Trust*, not a charity and an entirely separate company that funds projects often with a political dimension

royal, royalty l/c for royalty but cap *the Royal Family*; royal is usually l/c when used adjectivally, as in *royal baby, royal approval, the royal wave*, but takes the cap in titles such as *Royal Assent, Royal Collection, Royal Household, Royal Yacht*

Royal College of Nursing (not Nurses)

royal commissions should be capped when the full title is given, eg, *Royal Commission on Environmental Pollution*, but otherwise l/c, eg, *the royal commission*. See **committee**

Royal Corps of Signals, or **Royal Signals** (not Royal Corps of Signallers); see **Armed Forces** special section (page 164)

Royal Family takes caps, British and overseas; with names of the British Royal Family, give in full at first mention, eg, *the Duke of Edinburgh*, thereafter *the Duke* (cap) or occasionally *Prince Philip*; *Prince William*, thereafter *the Prince*. In royalty context, the cap after first mention should be confined to the British Royal Family and overseas heads of state. See **Queen, Duke, Prince, Diana, heads of state, Titles** special section (page 189)

Royal Fine Art Commission

Royal Fleet Auxiliary ships are entitled RFA, not HMS; eg, *RFA Fort George*. See **Armed Forces** special section (page 164)

Royal Institute of International Affairs (not Institution); often known as *Chatham House*

Royal Military Academy Sandhurst no commas; similarly *Royal Air Force College Cranwell* and *Royal Naval College Dartmouth*

Royal National Lifeboat Institution (not Life-Boat); abbreviate to RNLI

Royal Over-Seas League see **London clubs**

Royal Shakespeare Company thereafter the RSC; note also *Royal Opera House*; generally no need to include *Royal* with *Albert Hall*, *Festival Hall*, *National Theatre*

Royal Standard only for the Sovereign. Other members of the Royal Family have a *personal standard*; see **ensign**

Royal Train caps, as with the *Royal Yacht*

Royal Welch Fusiliers, The similarly, *Welch Regiment*; but note *Welsh Guards*; see **Armed Forces** special section (page 164)

Royal Yacht *Britannia*, or **the *Britannia*** she is now decommissioned, so refer to her as the *former Royal Yacht*

RPI retail prices index; note plural and l/c

RPM (caps), resale price maintenance (not retail); and *rpm* (l/c) revolutions per minute

RSPCA does not exist in Scotland, which has the Scottish SPCA

rubbish do not use as a verb

Rubens (Flemish painter; not Reubens)

Rue Royale see **French names**

run-down adjective, as in *decaying* or *exhausted*; note noun *rundown* as in briefing; also verb *to run down*

running-mate hyphen

Rural England Council for the Protection of Rural England (not Preservation); abbreviate to CPRE

rush hour noun; but note hyphen for adjective, eg, *rush-hour traffic*

rushed to hospital avoid this cliché. Use *taken to* or *driven to;* similarly, write a victim was *flown to hospital* rather than *airlifted to* … Always avoid the American *hospitalise*

Russia take care not to designate parts of the former Soviet Union as Russia when they no longer are, eg, Ukraine, Georgia. The same applies to the people (though there are millions of ethnic Russians throughout the former Soviet Union). So always specify the republic concerned and do not use *Russian* in the inclusive sense except in the phrase *Russian vodka*. Use *Soviet* and the *Soviet Union* only in their historical contexts – and avoid USSR wherever possible. See **Soviet**

Russian names use *i* as first name ending, but *y* for surnames, eg, *Arkadi Volsky*, *Gennadi Yavlinsky* (but note the exception *Rutskoi*); and use *k* rather than *x* in the middle, eg, *Aleksei*, *Aleksandr*; also note *Viktor*. We should use the *-ya* rather than *-ia* in *Natalya* and *Tatyana* (not Natalia, Tatiana). But note that the styles of Garry Kasparov and Anatoly Karpov are sufficiently Westernised to be spelt thus. See **chess names**

S...

saccharin (noun), **saccharine** (adjective)

sack avoid in the sense of *dismiss* except in headlines (and never use *axe* in this context)

sacrilegious (from sacrilege; not sacreligious)

Saddam Hussein, President write in full at first mention, then *Saddam*

Sadler's Wells

said prefer the construction *Mr Brown said* rather than *said Mr Brown*. See **writes**

sailing correspondent do not use yachting correspondent

Sainsbury the formal style is *J Sainsbury* (no point), especially in business stories, but *Sainsbury's* is permissible in general news stories. See **initials**

Saint nearly always abbreviated to *St*

St Albans

St Andrews (town and university in Fife)

St Catharine's College, Cambridge but note *St Catherine's College*, Oxford; see **Oxford University**, **Cambridge University**, **Catherine**

St David's (village and cathedral, Pembrokeshire); also St David's Head; but note the Bishop of St Davids does not take the apostrophe

St Giles' Cathedral, Edinburgh

St Helens, Merseyside

St James's Palace see **Court of...**

St John Ambulance Brigade/Association

St John's, Newfoundland but note **Saint John**, New Brunswick

St John's, Smith Square use comma

St John's Wood, London

St Katharine Docks, but *St Katharine's Yacht Haven*

St Martin-in-the-Fields

St Martins College of Art and Design see **Central St Martins**

St Neot, Cornwall but note **St Neots**, Cambridgeshire

St Paul's Cathedral

St Stephen's Green, Dublin (not Stephen's Green)

St Thomas' Hospital, London

Saint-Saëns (composer)

saleroom one word

Salonika, rather than Thessaloniki. See **foreign place names**

salutary not salutory

Salvadorean (not -ian)

Sam-7 (missiles)

Sanaa (capital of Yemen; not Sana'a, Sana, or other variants)

sanatorium (not sanitorium); note plural *sanatoriums*

sanction as a noun, define its use as trade, military etc

sandpit one word

SANE (schizophrenia charity); note caps

Santer, Jacques (former President of the European Commission); he is from Luxembourg, so call him Mr, not M; see **foreign appellations**

sarin (as in nerve gas); l/c

Sauchiehall Street, Glasgow

Saudi must never be used as short form for the country, Saudi Arabia. Confine its use to the adjectival, eg, *Saudi Royal Family*

Savile Row, Savile Club see **London clubs**

Savile, Jimmy use *Sir James* in formal context only

Saville Theatre

SBS Special Boat Service (not Squadron)

Sca Fell, Scafell Pike two separate mountains in the Lake District. Scafell Pike, at 3,206ft, is the highest in England

Scalextric (not Scalectrix)

Scandinavia (never Scandanavia)

Scarborough, North Yorkshire

scarify (to cut into, to cut skin from); its colloquial meaning of *to terrify* should be avoided wherever possible

scars do not heal (even metaphorically); *wounds* heal, *scars* remain

Schadenfreude (malicious enjoyment of another's misfortunes); note cap, italic

Schiphol airport, Amsterdam

schizophrenic never use as a term of abuse and avoid as a metaphor. See **medical terms, SANE**

Schleswig-Holstein

Schoenberg, Arnold

schools cap when full title is given (if in doubt, consult the *Independent Schools Year Book* or the state sector equivalent, the *Education Year Book*); nowadays use the classifications of *independent*, *state*, *grant-maintained*, *comprehensive*, *grammar*, *secondary modern* (rarely), etc, rather than public, private etc (except in historical context)

schoolchildren one word; note also *schoolgirl*, *schoolboy*, *schooldays*, *schoolmaster*, *schoolmistress* and *schoolteacher* (rarely), but *school-leaver*

School Curriculum and Assessment Authority (not Schools); but see **QCA**

Schwarzenegger, Arnold

Schweitzer, Albert

scientific measures write out first time with abbreviations in parentheses, shorten thereafter. The abbreviation takes no point and no *s* in the plural, eg, *14km* (not 14kms). Some basic international units and their abbreviations are: *metre* (*m*); *gram* (*g*); *litre* (*l*); *ampere* (*A*); *volt* (*V*); *watt* (*W*); note also *kilowatt-hour* (*kWh*).

Only abbreviate *mile* to *m* in *mph* and *mpg*; and *gallon* to *g* in *mpg* (otherwise *gal*). Beware of using *m* for million or for miles in any scientific context when it might be taken for metres. See **weights**

scientific names when employing the Latin terminology, use the internationally accepted convention of initial cap on the first (genus) word, then l/c for the second (species); eg, Homo sapiens, *Branta canadensis* (Canada goose) etc. Italicise all but the most common

Scilly, Isles of (not Scilly Isles); note spelling of *St Mary's* and *Tresco*

Scope new name for the former Spastics Society

Scotch (whisky); do not use as a substitute for the adjectives Scottish and Scots. But note *Scotch broth*, *Scotch mist*, *Scotch egg* and *Scotch terrier*; also *Scots pine*

Scottish National Party (SNP); now cap *Nationalists* in the Scottish party context, but l/c nationalists in the wider sense

Scottish place names always write, eg, Motherwell, North Lanarkshire (never Motherwell, Scotland). Take care with new names under local government reorganisation; regions such as *Central*, *Grampian* and *Strathclyde* should now be referred to only in their historical context or if they persist in official titles such as *Strathclyde Police* or *the University of Strathclyde*. Permissible too to refer informally to the

Central belt (between Edinburgh and Glasgow).

The same principle about counties applies to Wales and Northern Ireland: give the county unless the town or city is big enough or well-known enough for the county to be unnecessary

Scottish Parliament now cap *P*. Note First Minister (not Secretary)

ScottishPower

Scott Thomas, Kristin (no hyphen)

Scouts no longer Boy Scouts

scrapheap one word

scratchcard one word; similarly *smartcard, swipecard*

Scripture cap as in *Holy Scripture*; but note l/c *scriptural*

scriptwriter

sculptures set in italic. With photographs of sculptures, always give the sculptor's name. See **Arts** special section (page 169)

seabed, seabird, seahorse, seagull, seasick no hyphens

seasonal, but **unseasonable** (not unseasonal). Note also *seasonal affective disorder* (l/c), abbreviated to SAD

seasons always l/c when unattached, ie, *spring, summer, autumn, winter*; but note *Winter Olympics* etc

seatbelt

second-hand hyphenated

Second World War (not World War II/Two etc)

Secret Intelligence Service abbreviate to SIS, or MI6; takes caps; see **Security Service** (MI5)

Secretary-General (of the United Nations, Nato)

Securities and Investments Board the SIB has now been replaced by the new City super-regulator, the *Financial Services Authority* (FSA)

Security Service (MI5); takes caps; but l/c for *security services* in non-specific use. See **Secret Intelligence Service**

seize (never sieze)

select committees as with parliamentary committees cap at first mention, or when full title is given, eg, *the Foreign Affairs Select Committee*; thereafter *the select committee*, or *the committee*

Selfridges

sell-off, sell-out but see **buyout**

Sellotape trade name, so cap; alternatively use *sticky tape* or *adhesive tape*

semiconductor

Semtex cap

Senate (US); write *Senator Edward Kennedy*, thereafter *the senator*; alternatively, *Mr Kennedy, the Massachusetts senator*

senior abbreviate to *Sr* (not Snr) in the American context, eg, *Henry Ramstein Sr*; see **junior**. Avoid the cliché *senior executive* when you mean *executive* – nine times out of ten the adjective is redundant (as *major*)

Senior Salaries Review Body caps; has replaced the Top Salaries Review Body

septuagenarian

Serb for the people, but *Serbian* can be used (sparingly) as an adjective

Serious Fraud Office abbreviate to SFO; but note *fraud squad*. See **Flying Squad**

Serjeant at Arms

Serps spell out at first mention as *state earnings related pension scheme (Serps)*

serve in a warship (but *on* a merchant ship), and serve in (not on) a submarine, even though subs are boats, not ships. Important to make this distinction. See **Armed Forces** special section (page 164)

Services, Armed Services, or **Armed Forces, the** note caps; also cap *Service* when used adjectivally as in *a Service family* (where meaning might otherwise be ambiguous); but l/c *serviceman, servicewoman*

Session, Court of (supreme Scottish court; not Sessions). See **Courts** special section (page 176)

setback noun; but note *to set back*

sett as with badgers

set-up try to find a synonym such as *arrangement, organisation, structure, system* etc

sewage (waste matter); note **sewerage** (disposal system)

sexism always be aware of sensitivities and be careful to avoid giving offence to women. It is often difficult to draw the line between sexism and political correctness

sex offenders register (l/c, no apostrophe)

Shadow cap in all cases, such as *Shadow Cabinet, Shadow Environment Secretary, Shadow Chief Whip, a Shadow spokesman.* See **Politics** special section (page 181)

Shah, Eddy (not Eddie)

shake-out, shake-up but see **buyout**

Shakespearean (not -ian)

shall, should keep up the vigorous defence of these against the encroaching *will* and *would.* Good practice is that *shall* and *should* go with the first person singular and plural (I shall, we shall), *will* and *would* with the others (he will, they will). *Shall* with second and third persons singular and plural has a slightly more emphatic meaning than *will*

shambles take care not to overwork this strong word, which means a *slaughterhouse* and, by extension, a *scene of carnage*

Shankill Road, Belfast (not Shankhill); see **Ireland**

Shangri-La

SHAPE Supreme Headquarters, Allied Powers, Europe; all caps

share a joke banned in captions on photographs showing people laughing

share shop(s) l/c, as jobcentre

Sharia (Islamic law); never use the tautology *Sharia law*

sheikh (not shaikh)

Shepherds Bush

Sherborne alumni of the Dorset public school are *Shirburnians*

sheriff (never sherrif)

Shetland, or **the Shetland Islands** (not the Shetlands). See **Orkney**

Shia (not Shiite or any such variation); write *Shia Muslims* (as opposed to *Sunni Muslims*)

ships italicise the HMS when first mention of warship, eg, *HMS Sheffield.* Ships should generally be treated as feminine; thus *she* and *her* rather than *it* and *its.* See **warships, boat, serve in**

ships' tonnage for passenger ships, give gross tonnage in *tonnes* (rather than tons); for cargo ships, deadweight tonnage. Check with *Lloyd's Register*

shock avoid in headlines unless in the electric context; in text, use the word as little as possible and never as a modifier, *shock revelations* etc (unless the context is ironic)

shock waves two words, but use sparingly as a metaphor as it is becoming a cliché

shopkeeper, shopowner, shopfront, shoplift etc but note *shop assistant* and *shop steward*

shortlist one word as noun or verb

short-lived, short-sighted

showbusiness one word; note *showbiz* is acceptable in quotes and informal context

showcase avoid use as a verb *to showcase something*. Use *display* or *exhibit* instead

showjumping should now be one word except when it appears in a title such as the *British Show Jumping Association*, or the name of an event using it as two words; similarly, *showjumper*

Shroud of Turin, or **the Turin Shroud** note caps; subsequently *the shroud* (l/c)

Siamese cats, twins for Siam use Thailand except in historical context; note the adjective Thai

Sichuan (not Szechuan, Setzuan, Szechwan or any other variant); see **Chinese names**

sickbed similarly *deathbed*

side-effects

siege (never seige)

Siena (not Sienna)

sign language (not deaf-and-dumb language)

Silicon Valley, silicon chips, but *silicone implants* (for breasts etc)

silk barristers *take silk* and *become silks* (all l/c); see **Courts** special section (page 176)

Simon's Town, South Africa (not Simonstown); see **South Africa**

Sindy doll (not Cindy)

singeing (from *singe*), to distinguish it from *singing*

sink, sank the past participle is *sunk*, the adjective *sunken*

siphon (not syphon)

Sistine Chapel (not Cistine)

sitcom permissible abbreviation for *situation comedy*

sit-in

situation avoid wherever possible; such phrases as *crisis situation, ongoing situation* and *no-win situation* are banned unless a direct quote demands them

Six Nations Championship (rugby), no longer the Five Nations Championship (England, Wales, Scotland, Ireland, France and Italy)

sizeable

ski, skier, skied, skiing

skulduggery

Slavic must not be used; the noun and adjective are *Slav*

slay do not use this biblical word in headlines for *kill* or *murder*

slimline one word

Slovak (people and language); *Slovakian* is the general adjective. See **Croat**

smartcard one word; similarly *scratchcard, swipecard*

smelt (not smelled)

Smith, WH no points; see **companies, initials**

Smithsonian Institution, Washington (never Institute); can be shortened to *the Smithsonian*

snarl-up do not use as a synonym of *traffic jam, confusion* etc

sniffer dogs, tracker dogs avoid these clichés wherever possible; usually *dogs* is sufficient, but if the context is unclear, write *police dogs*

snowball, snowbound, snowdrift, snowfall, snowman etc

Soane's the museum in Lincoln's Inn Fields is *the Sir John Soane's Museum*

soap opera prefer to just *soap*, though the latter may have its place in less formal pieces

soccer an acceptable word. See **football** and **Sports** special section (page 185)

social chapter l/c, as it is an informal title

Social Democratic and Labour Party (Northern Ireland); abbreviate to SDLP

socialism, socialist for when to cap, see **communism**

Solent, the note l/c *the*

Solicitor-General hyphen, as *Attorney-General*; similarly *Solicitor-General for Scotland*

Solicitors Complaints Bureau no apostrophes; has now been replaced by the *Office for the Supervision of Solicitors*

Solti, Sir Georg (not George)

Solzhenitsyn, Aleksandr no longer use Anglicised spelling; see **Russian names**

SOS

Sotheby's

soundbite

south, southeast, southern etc for when to cap, see **compass points**

South Africa never use the abbreviation SA, even in headlines.
The capital is Pretoria, which has the embassies (branches sometimes in Cape Town when Parliament is sitting) and government ministries. The legislature meets in Cape Town, and the Appeal Court sits in Bloemfontein. Pretoria can be referred to as the seat of government. Each of the new South African provinces has its own capital.
Note caps for *Northern Province* and the *Eastern/ Western/ Northern Cape, KwaZulu/ Natal* and *Simon's Town*.
Take care; several provinces have been renamed since the apartheid era, eg, *Mpumalanga* (formerly Eastern Transvaal). Use *southern Africa* when referring to Africa south of the Congo and Zambezi Rivers

South Asia encompasses Afghanistan, Bangladesh, Bhutan, India, the Maldives, Nepal, Pakistan and Sri Lanka

South-East Asia comprises the nine Asean states – Indonesia, Singapore, Malaysia, Thailand, the Philippines, Brunei, Vietnam, Burma and Laos – plus Cambodia. Avoid calling Burma *Myanmar* (except occasionally in direct quotes). See **Asean**

South of France

Southern Ocean caps

Sovereign, the cap; see **monarch, Royal Family**

Soviet Union never refer to *the Soviets* for the people or the Government, even in the historical context. The phrase is an Americanism often with disparaging overtones; a *soviet* is a *committee*, not a person. Refer instead to *the Soviet people* or *the Soviet Government* in historical context. See **Russia, USSR**

space avoid the phrase *outer space*; see **Earth, Moon, Sun, Universe**

Spanish regions use the Anglicised forms such as *Andalusia* (not Andalucía); *Catalonia* (not Cataluña), *Navarre* (not Navarra), *Majorca* (not Mallorca), *Minorca* (not Menorca) etc

spastic never use figuratively or as a term of abuse; see **medical terms, Scope**

Speaker always cap in parliamentary context

Special Branch caps, but no *the*; see **branch**

species both singular and plural in plant and animal sense. See **scientific names**

spelt (not spelled); note *misspelt*

Spiceworld: the Movie

spiders note they are not insects, although like insects they are arthropods

Spielberg, Steven

spilt (not spilled)

spin, spun (do not use *span* as past tense)

spin-doctor hyphen; see **Politics** special section (page 181)

Spiritualism, Spiritualist

split infinitives do not use except in famous quotes such as "to boldly go where no man . . ." or in limited emphatic constructions such as "I want to live – to really live"

spoilt (not spoiled); but note *despoiled*

spokesman, spokeswoman avoid where possible, eg, "the ministry said" rather than "a ministry spokesman said". *Official* is a useful alternative. Never use *spokesperson*. See **chairman**

sports clubs for when to use singular or plural, see **teams**

sportsmen, sportswomen omit the Mr, Mrs, Miss, Ms etc unless they are in news reports (eg, court hearings) in a specifically non-sporting context. See **appellations**

sprang (past tense of the verb *to spring*, eg, "she sprang into action"); note *sprung* (past participle, eg, "the wind has sprung up")

sprightly (not spritely)

spring-clean hyphen

squads in police context, usually l/c, but see **Flying Squad;** also note **Royal and Diplomatic Protection Squad**

Sri Lanka do not use Ceylon for the country except in historical context. But note *Ceylon tea* etc

SSSI site of special scientific interest, l/c

stadium plural *stadiums*; see **referendum**

stalemate try to avoid in the sense of *deadlock*. It should be confined to chess reports

Stalinist, Stalinism see **communism**

stanch verb, as in *to stanch a flow of blood*; note adjective *staunch* meaning *loyal* or *firm*

stand-off noun, hyphen; but note **standby**, noun, no hyphen

Stansted (airport; never Stanstead); see **airports**

stargazers, stargazing

Star Trek two words, italic

State cap; use sparingly in context of the State as a wide concept; but l/c in the *welfare state*, or when used adjectivally, eg, *state benefits*

stationary (not moving); but **stationery** (writing materials)

Stationery Office, The (TSO abbreviated); no longer HMSO

stations l/c in *Euston station, Waterloo station, Birmingham New Street station*, but where possible, simply *Euston, Waterloo* etc. See **airports**

statistic(s) do not use as a fancy word for *figure(s)* or *number(s)*. Note that the Central Statistical Office has been replaced by the *Office for National Statistics* (not of)

status quo roman; but note italics for the less familiar *status quo ante*

statute book

stay home avoid; use *stay at home* instead

Stealth bomber

steelworks, steelworker etc

stepfather, stepmother, stepson, stepdaughter but note *step-family*, *step-parents*

Stephenson, George (trains), **Robert** (bridges) note also **Stevenson**, Robert Louis, Adlai

still avoid writing the tautologous "still continues", "still remains" etc

Stock Exchange caps for *London Stock Exchange* and *New York Stock Exchange*, l/c for all others; note l/c for **stock market**

stony (not stoney)

storey (of a building); note plural *storeys*

storyteller, storytelling

straight be sparing in the use of this word to mean heterosexual. See **gay**

straight-faced but note **straightforward**

Strait of Hormuz, Strait of Gibraltar, Strait of Dover (not Straits)

straitjacket

strait-laced note also *in dire straits*

Stratford-upon-Avon except in the parliamentary constituency, which is *Stratford-on-Avon*

stratum plural *strata*

Streisand, Barbra

stress prefer *emphasise* as in "he emphasised the importance"

stricture means *adverse criticism* or *censure* (not constraint)

strippagram

stylebook one word, as with *guidebook*, *textbook* etc; but note *style guide*

sub- like *multi-*, the hyphen here is often a question of what looks better. A random sample gives us *subdivision*, *sublet*, *subnormal*, *subsection*, *substandard*, *subtext*; in contrast, *sub-committee*,

sub-editor, sub-postmaster, sub-post office etc. See **hyphens, multi-**
Subbuteo

sub-continent, the (India, Pakistan and Bangladesh); note l/c

subjects, academic use l/c for most subjects studied at school or university, eg, "she was reading modern history with philosophy"; but where a proper name is involved, the cap is retained, eg, "he got a first in English literature and German after he dropped Latin in his second year"; and always cap Classics and PPE (short for philosophy, politics and economics). But note, eg, Professor of History when the phrase accompanies a name; see **Professor, university posts**

sub-let (as in property)

sub-machinegun see **machinegun**

submarine always a *boat*, not a ship. See **boat, ships, serve in**

subplot, subtext, subtitle

subpoena, subpoenas, subpoenaing, subpoenaed

sub-Saharan Africa

subsequently prefer *afterwards* or *later*, and never say *subsequent to* when the meaning is *after*

subtropical one word; see **Tropics**

such as do not confuse with *like*; see **like**

Sudan (not the Sudan, except occasionally in historical context)

suing (from *to sue*; not sueing)

summon the verb is *to summon*, the noun *a summons* (plural *summonses*). A person is *summoned* to appear before a tribunal etc; but a person in receipt of a specific summons can be said to have been *summonsed*. But see **Woolf reforms** and **Courts** special section (page 176)

Sun see **Earth, Moon** and **Universe**

sunbathing, sunburn, sunglasses, suntan etc but note *sun-care* (products etc)

superhighway (as in information superhighway); similarly *superconductor*

superlatives beware of calling any person, event or thing *the first, the biggest, the best* etc without firm evidence that this is correct. Also, never say *first-ever, best-ever* etc; see **ever, first, universal claims**

supersede (never supercede)

supersonic (of speeds); for waves use *ultrasonic*

supervisor (not superviser)

supine (lying face-up); see **prone**

Supreme Court (US)

Surinam (not Suriname)

surprising (not suprising)

Sussex always specify whether a place is in East Sussex or West Sussex, two separate counties

swap (not swop). Do not use unless a mutual exchange is involved and never for organ transplants

swaths (as in *cutting swaths through*; not *swathes*); note **swathes** to be used only as bandages

swatting (flies), **swotting** (study)

swearword

swingeing (as in cuts), to distinguish it from *swinging*

Swinging London, Swinging Sixties caps

swipecard similarly *scratchcard, smartcard*

Symphony Hall, Birmingham (does not take *the*). See **Arts** special section (page 169)

synod l/c on its own, but note caps for *General Synod*. See **Churches** special section (page 172)

synthesizer (musical); but note **synthesise** (chemical etc)

T...

-t in nearly all cases, where there is a choice of past tense between a final *-t* or *-ed*, use *-t*, as in *burnt, spelt* etc. But never *earnt*

tad heavily overworked as synonym of *a little* or *a bit*; avoid

T

tailback

Tajikistan

takeaway (meals)

take-off (aircraft)

takeover noun; but note verb *to take over*

takeover code but note caps for *Takeover Panel*

Taleban (Afghan Islamic rebel group) takes a singular verb; no need to say *the* Taleban unless appropriate; note that the singular is *a Taleb*, but prefer *a member of Taleban*

talk show similarly *chat show, game show, quiz show* etc

Tallinn (capital of Estonia)

Tangier no final *s*

Tannoy trade name, so cap; use *loudspeaker* as alternative

Taoiseach always cap; see **Ireland**

taramasalata (not taramo-); see **hoummos**

targeted

Tarmac trade name, but cap *T* is used only for the civil engineering company. Common usage allows the road surface or airport runway to be written as *tarmac*; *tarmacadam* is not a trade name

Tartars preferred to Tatars

task force (as in Falklands)

tattoos, tattooed, tattooing

taxman one word as colloquialism for *Inland Revenue*; similarly taxpayer

Tchaikovsky

teams normally plural, eg, "Manchester United were disappointing when they lost to Barcelona". But sports clubs usually take the singular, especially in news stories, eg, "Manchester City Football Club was fined heavily for crowd disturbances". There is some room for variation in this format, but whatever is decided, never mix singular and plural in the same story. Note hyphen in *team-mates*. See **Sports** special section (page 185)

teargas

Technicolor trade name. It must not be used except in that company's context. Use *multicoloured* as the general alternative

Tecs short for training and enterprise councils; note initial cap only; see **Lecs**

Teesside no hyphen, double *s* in middle; but note *Deeside* in both Scotland and Wales

teetotal

Tehran (not Teheran)

telephone numbers with three groups of figures, hyphenate only the first two, eg, 0181-234 8464. With revised codes (introduced in June 1999, but not fully operational until April 2000) write, eg, 020-7782 5000, not 0207-782 5000.

Teletext replaced Oracle (at the end of 1992) as the text service for ITV and Channel 4; do not use Oracle any more

television use TV in headlines, but try to avoid in the text. ITV is an acceptable alternative for *independent television*. ITN (Independent Television News) is acceptable in its abbreviated form (in the same way as BBC). Note l/c in non-specific use, eg, *BBC Television*, *BBC1*, *BBC2* etc; but *Argentine television*, *Norwegian television* etc. See **BBC**, **ITV**, **Channel 4**, **Radio 1**

television and radio programmes italicise, except for first mention in reviews, when they go in bold. See **Arts** special section (page 169)

temperatures the style is *16C (61F)*. See **celsius**

ten-minute rule (Bill) etc; see **Politics** special section (page 181)

Tennessee

tenpin bowling

Teresa see **Mother**

Terminal 1 (Heathrow; also Terminal 2, 3, 4, 5 etc). See **airports**, **Heathrow**

Terre'Blanche, Eugene

Terrence Higgins Trust (not Terence)

Territorial Army, or **the Territorials** note cap *T*

terrorist take care with this word and the associated *terrorism*; *guerrilla* is a less loaded word in the context of violent political struggle. Never use as a synonym of any dissident group that uses violence, eg, *hunt saboteurs*, and always try to specify groups as *paramilitaries, gangster organisations* etc. Remember, one man's terrorist is another man's freedom fighter

Tessa(s) tax-exempt special savings account

Test match should apply only to *cricket* (not rugby); for other sports, use the term *international* (match). See **Sports** special section (page 185)

textbook one word, similarly *guidebook, stylebook, rulebook* etc

TGV (*train à grande vitesse* – not *de*; French high-speed train)

thalidomide l/c

Thames Barrier, Thames Estuary caps; see **rivers**

Thamesmead, near Erith note *Thamesdown* (Wiltshire administrative district), but *Thames-side*

that do not be shy of this word after *said, denied, claimed* etc; eg, "he denied that the evidence was confusing" is more elegant than "he denied the evidence was confusing". *That* is almost always better than *which* in a defining clause, eg, "the train that I take stops at Slough". As a general rule, use *which* for descriptive clauses and place it between commas, eg, "the night train, which used to carry newspapers, stops at Crewe". See **ensure**

Thatcher at first mention Baroness Thatcher, thereafter Lady Thatcher. In historical context, preferable to say Mrs Thatcher or Margaret Thatcher, eg, "Mrs Thatcher took quick action in sending the task force to the Falklands". It would be wrong to say that her party forced Lady Thatcher from office in 1990. Note **Sir Denis Thatcher** (not Dennis)

theatre always attach *Theatre* (cap) to names at first mention, eg, *the Criterion Theatre* (thereafter *the Criterion* or simply *the theatre*). Some of the main London exceptions are *the Old Vic, Young Vic, Palladium, Coliseum, Apollo Victoria, Donmar Warehouse, Hackney Empire*; and outside London, many such as the *Birmingham Hippodrome, Oxford Playhouse, West Yorkshire Playhouse* etc. See **Arts** special section (page 169)

theatregoer

the then avoid expressions such as "the then Prime Minister" or (worse) "the then Mr Callaghan"; write "then Prime Minister", "who was Prime Minister at the time" or "Lord Callaghan of Cardiff (then Mr Callaghan)"

The Times almost always use italics for the name of the newspaper, except in headlines. But Times Newspapers Ltd (roman), publisher of *The Times* and *The Sunday Times,* is the operating company of Times Newspapers Holdings.

Also (especially in features headlines, standfirsts etc) The Times Gardener etc is an acceptable style to avoid a mass of italics and apostrophes.

In text, in the difficult area of correspondents' and executive titles, it is permissible to say "the *Times* political correspondent", "the *Times* wine correspondent" etc, although "political editor of *The Times*", "wine correspondent of *The Times*" etc are preferable.

Always say "Editor of *The Times*", "deputy editor of *The Times*" etc.

It is permissible to say "a *Times* reader", "*Times* readers", but prefer "readers of *The Times*". Similarly, adjectival uses such as "a *Times* article", "a *Times* offer" are acceptable.

Also note Times Law Report (without *The*), but *The Times* Diary, *The Times* Crossword etc. Again, some flexibility – to avoid a proliferation of italics – can be used in puff material etc.

For sections of the paper, avoid italics: eg, *The Times* Magazine, Weekend, Interface.

Keep phrases such as "told *The Times*" to a minimum: *said* is usually preferable.

Note supplements: *The Times Educational Supplement, The Times Higher Education Supplement, The Times Literary Supplement,* and *Nursery World.*

See **correspondents, editor, exclusive, News International**

thermonuclear

Thermos trade name, so always cap

they should always agree with the subject. Avoid sentences such as "If someone loves animals, they should protect them". Say instead "If people love animals, they should protect them"

think-tanks take care in describing their ideological persuasions; we should call the Social Market Foundation (SMF), Demos and Politeia *independent think-tanks*; the Centre for Policy Studies (CPS) and the Institute of Economic Affairs (IEA) *free-market* or *right-wing think-tanks*; and the Institute for Public Policy Research (IPPR) a *left-wing think-tank*

Third Way (caps); new Labour's political stratagem

Third World (caps)

This Morning, the Richard (Madeley) and Judy (Finnegan) show (not *This Morning with Richard and Judy*)

threshold

throne cap sparingly, only in terms of the institution, eg, "he deferred to the wisdom of the Throne"; in other contexts, as with the chair itself, use l/c, eg, "The Queen came to the throne in 1952"

thunderbolts are mythological and do not exist; *lightning bolts* and *thunderclaps* do exist and can also be used metaphorically

thus far avoid; prefer *so far*

Tiananmen Square, Beijing

"tiger" economies (of South-East Asia and the Pacific); use quotes where possible for first mention, subsequently without quotes, and always l/c

time bomb but note *timescale, timeshare*

times never write 6pm last night, 9am tomorrow morning; instead write *6 o'clock last night* or (if the context allows) *6pm*, or *9am tomorrow*

Tinseltown (as in Hollywood); one word

titles the most common solecism is to write Lady Helen Brown etc when we should say simply *Lady Brown*. As a quick rule of thumb, no wife of a baronet or knight takes her Christian name in her title unless she is the daughter of a duke, marquess or earl.

Some titles include a place name, eg, Lord Callaghan of Cardiff, Lord Archer of Weston-super-Mare, while others do not. Follow *Who's Who*, where those whose place name must be included appear in bold caps.

Always check with *Debrett* or *Who's Who* if in doubt. See **Titles** special section (page 189)

together with avoid; prefer simply *with*; also beware such tautology as *blend together, meet together, link together* etc

Tolkien, J.R.R. (not Tolkein)

tomatoes plural; similarly *potatoes*

tons, tonnes prefer to use *tonnes* in most contexts, though in historical passages *tons* would be more appropriate

Tontons Macoute (Haiti); plural, no final *s*

Top Salaries Review Body now called the *Senior Salaries Review Body*

Top Ten, Top 20, Top 40 etc (in musical or other lists)

tornado (storm); plural *tornados*; also *Tornado, Tornados* (aircraft)

torpedo but note plural *torpedoes*

Torvill (Jayne) **and Dean** (Christopher)

Tory, Tories acceptable alternative for *Conservative(s)*. Note *Tory party* (l/c *p*) is permissible. See **Conservative, committee** (for 1922 Committee), **select committees**, and **Politics** special section (page 181)

totalisator, tote take l/c, no quotes; note *the Tote* refers to the organisation

touchpaper

towards (not toward)

townhouse (one word)

tracker dogs, sniffer dogs avoid these clichés wherever possible; usually *dogs* is sufficient, but if the context is unclear, say *police dogs*

tracksuit one word

Trade Descriptions Act

trade-in noun or adjective; but note verb *to trade in*

trademark (one word)

trade names many names of products in common use are proprietary and must be given a capital letter (at risk of legal action if we fail to do so); eg, *Biro, CinemaScope, Dictaphone, Hoover, Jeep, Kodak, Land Rover, Lycra, Perspex, Polaroid, Rollerblade, Tannoy, Technicolor, Thermos, Walkman, Xerox, Yale lock*. Be especially careful about drugs: try to use non-proprietary words such as *aspirin, sleeping pills* etc

trade unions plural (not trades unions); but note *Trades Union Congress*. See **TUC**

trainspotter, trainspotting no hyphens

tranquilliser, tranquillity

transatlantic, transcontinental but note *cross-Channel*

transistor do not use on its own in sense of *transistor radio*

transpire (*to come to light* or *to leak out*). Do not use as an alternative of *to happen* or *occur*

transsexual no hyphen; but note *trans-ship*

Transvaal but note *a Transvaler*; see **South Africa**

trauma, traumatic avoid in the clichéd sense of *deeply upsetting,* *distressing* etc; it should be confined to its medical meaning of severe shock after an accident or stressful event

travellers, New Age travellers see **Gypsy, hippy**

traveller's cheques

Travellers Club no apostrophe; see **London clubs**

Triads cap in Chinese gangster context

Tricolour cap for the French flag, l/c in more general context

trillion American for *a thousand billion* (or *a million million*, 1,000,000,000,000), and should be explained as such in stories about overseas budgets, for example. Try to avoid in stories about Britain

Trinity College Dublin no comma

triple crown (rugby). See **Sports** special section (page 185)

tripos l/c general context, but note *the History Tripos* etc

trolleys plural of trolley (not -ies)

Trooping the Colour (not *of* the Colour); note also *beating retreat*

Tropics, the cap; note also *the Tropic of Capricorn/ Cancer*, but l/c *tropical, subtropical*

Troubles, the see **Ireland**

troubleshooter one word; similarly *troublespot*

truck permissible in most contexts; see **lorry**

Truman, Harry S. (former US President), but **Fred Trueman**, cricketer

try to the verb *try* must be followed by *to* before the next verb, never by *and,* eg, "I will try to cross the road", not "I will try and cross the road"

Tsar (not czar); also *Tsarevich, Tsaritsa* (not czarina); caps with the name, l/c in general sense. But note the exception *drugs czar*

TSA The Securities Association

TSB formerly the Trustee Savings Bank, now part of Lloyds TSB

T-shirt

Tube cap; acceptable in context on its own for *London Tube*, or *London Underground*. Also cap the various lines such as *Central Line, Metropolitan Line, Victoria Line* etc

tuberculosis the adjective is *tuberculous* (not tubercular)

TUC Trades Union Congress. Note at first mention *General Council of the TUC*, thereafter *general council*. Cap also *General Secretary of the TUC* (as leader of the national body), but note l/c *general secretaries* of individual unions

tug-of-war

tunku (Malaysian prince); cap before name, otherwise l/c

turbo-jet, turbo-prop see **aircraft**

Turin Shroud subsequently *the shroud*

Turkey cap parties, as in *Motherland Party*, *Welfare Party*, *True Path Party* etc

turn down prefer *reject* or *refuse* (except of beds)

turnlines in bold, set right on the front page (and on inside pages where the story begins and spills) – eg, **Continued on page 2, col 7** – and set left on inside pages, eg, **Continued from page 1**

turn-off, turn-on nouns, but note no hyphens in *turnout*, *turnaround*, *turnabout*

Tussaud's, Madame but note *the Tussauds Group* (no apostrophe), which also includes *the London Planetarium*, *Warwick Castle*, *Alton Towers* and *Chessington World of Adventures*.

Tutankhamun never permit a break as Tutan-khamun; if the name has to be broken on a turn, it may be hyphenated as *Tut-ankhamun* or *Tutankh-amun*

Tutsis see **Hutus**

TV-am no longer exists

Twentieth Century Fox

twentysomething, thirtysomething, fortysomething etc if this modern cliché must be used

Twin Towers (of Wembley) (caps)

twofold, threefold, fourfold, tenfold etc

two minutes' silence, the see **Armistice, Remembrance**

two thirds, three quarters etc but hyphenate adjectival use, eg, *a two-thirds share*. Such expressions usually take the plural verb, eg, "three quarters of the children prefer horror films"; the same applies even in "a third of the children prefer blancmange". But note "two thirds of the bus was empty"

Tyne and Wear (not &)

typify, typified (not typefy)

Tyrol (no longer Tirol)

U...

U no full point after Burmese prefix, eg, U Nu

Ucas Universities and Colleges Admissions Service (not UCAS)

Uefa, Uefa Cup (not UEFA); see **Cup, Sports** special section (page 185)

UK acceptable abbreviation for *United Kingdom* in both text and headlines. But be careful that it is strictly applicable; see **Britain**

Ukraine (not *the* Ukraine)

Ulster permissible, especially in headlines, but use *Northern Ireland* or *the Province* when possible; see **Ireland**

ultimate use sparingly. *Ultimate limit* means *limit*

ultimatums (not ultimata); see **referendum**

ultraviolet

unchristian l/c; see **Christian**

uncoordinated but note *co-ordinate*; see **hyphens**

under-age hyphenated; similarly *over-age*

underestimate

Underground, London see **Tube**

underreact

undervalue

underwater one word as adjective, eg, *underwater exploration*; but two words as adverb, eg, the couple were married *under water*

under way always two words

Unesco United Nations Educational, Scientific, and Cultural

Organisation. See **United Nations**

UNHCR United Nations High Commissioner for Refugees. See **United Nations** (paragraph d)

Unionist cap in Ulster political context; see **Ireland**

Union Jack except in most naval and some ceremonial contexts, when **Union Flag** is correct; note that in the Royal Navy, *Union Jack* only when flown at the jackstaff

unique (only one, having no like or equal); do not use except in this specific sense. Phrases such as *very unique, even more unique* are nonsense and are banned

unitary authorities since the abolition of Avon, Humberside, Cleveland, and now Hereford and Worcester, plus wholesale reorganisation of Welsh and Scottish local government, take care when locating towns in these areas.

Former county of Avon: should now be described as in either Gloucestershire or Somerset.

Former Hereford and Worcester County Council: from April 1998, replaced by a new Worcestershire County Council and a new unitary authority for Herefordshire.

Former Berkshire County Council: replaced by six unitary authorities (Bracknell Forest, Newbury, Reading, Slough, Windsor and Maidenhead, and Wokingham).

Former Humberside: should be located as either East Riding (north of the Humber) or Lincolnshire (south of the river).

Former Cleveland, reorganised Yorkshire: cap the West and South in West Yorkshire and South Yorkshire, even though they are not new unitary authorities (as North Yorkshire is). The reason is that they are still regarded by people living there as cohesive regions, similar to the West Midlands and Greater Manchester, two other metropolitan counties that no longer exist per se. Moreover, statutory bodies such as *West Yorkshire Police* and *West Yorkshire Passenger Transport Authority* still exist; so the best rule-of-thumb will be to use the cap in future in all cases.

Wales: note that Clwyd, Dyfed and Gwent no longer exist as authorities, so unless the new county has a traditional and generally familiar name (eg, Pembrokeshire, Carmarthenshire, Powys, Denbighshire etc), it will often be simpler to locate smaller towns and villages just as in North Wales, Mid Wales, West Wales, South Wales. Note that Gwynedd does still exist as a unitary authority (though smaller than when it was a county). If in doubt, use one of the North/Mid/West/South designations.

Scotland: regions such as Central, Grampian and Strathclyde should now be referred to only in their historical context or if they persist in titles such as *Strathclyde Police* or *University of Strathclyde*. Permissible too to refer informally to the *Central belt* (between Edinburgh and Glasgow), despite the scrapping of Central region

United Nations, or **UN, the** spell out at first mention where possible, though this can no longer be a hard and fast rule. Other points:
a. *Secretary-General of the UN*; now Kofi Annan
b. *UN Security Council, UN General Assembly* at first mention, and thereafter keep the caps, as in *the Security Council, the General Assembly*
c. UN derivatives such as *Unesco, Unifil, Unprofor* etc are written thus where the word can be voiced. See **initials**
d. *The UN High Commissioner for Refugees* (never Commission) is the organisation, as well as a person. Abbreviate to UNHCR after first mention

United Reformed Church (not Reform); see **Churches** special section (page 172)

United States (of America); always followed by a singular verb. Common usage allows abbreviation to US in text as well as headlines, but do not ignore the word *America*. See **America(n)**, **New York**, **Washington**

universal claims always beware of claiming that something is the first or last of its kind, or that someone is the first person to ... or the last surviving member of ... or the oldest inhabitant etc. See **ever**, **first**, **superlatives**

Universe cap in planetary context, as *Sun, Earth, Moon* etc, but l/c in phrases such as "she became the centre of his universe"

universities always cap as in *Birmingham University* (or the *University of Birmingham*), *Sussex University, the University of East Anglia* etc; thereafter l/c *the university* . If in doubt about the proper title, consult *The Times Good University Guide*. See **Cambridge University**, **Oxford University**, **Vice-Chancellor**

University College London no comma

university posts at first mention, cap *Vice-Chancellor, Chancellor, Pro-Vice-Chancellor, Pro-Chancellor, Dean, Master, Professor, Fellow* etc; at subsequent mentions l/c; eg, "Dr Mark Blodkin, Professor of Modern History at Kent University, said ..." then later, "the professor said ..."

unlikeable, unloveable

unmistakable (not with the middle *e*)

unparalleled

unshakeable

Untouchables (in Indian caste system); cap

unveil take care with this word, which means to remove a covering from something, or (by extension) to disclose. It should not be used in phrases such as unveiling a ship, or unveiling a flag

up avoid unnecessary use after verbs, as in meet up, rest up, end up. See **down**

upbeat, upfront, upgrade

upmarket similarly *downmarket*

upon take care with use of *up, upon, up on,* and *on,* eg, "The cat jumped *on* the floor, *upon* the mouse, *up on* the table, then *up* the tree"

Upper House, Lower House see **Politics** special section (page 181)

Uruguay Round (world trade deal); note caps. See **Gatt, World Trade Organisation**

US see **America(n), United States**

USSR avoid wherever possible; write *Soviet Union* instead (and now only in historical context). See **Russia**

utilise almost always prefer *use*

Utopia, Utopian cap

U-turn overworked phrase, especially in the political context. Be sparing in its use, particularly when only a minor change of policy direction is involved

V...

vacuum in common use as a verb, but avoid *Hoover,* a trade name. See **Hoover, trade names**

vagaries means *aimless wanderings* or *eccentric ideas,* not *vicissitudes* or *changes* (as in weather)

Valentine's Day (normally omit St); keep cap for *Valentine card* etc

Valium proprietary term, so cap

Valletta (Malta)

valley cap in full name, such as *the Thames Valley, the Wye Valley* etc. Note also the *Welsh Valleys*

Van cap in Dutch names when surname alone is given, eg, Van Gogh, but l/c when used in full, eg, Vincent van Gogh. Note Ludwig *van* Beethoven (not von), although the composer was German. See **von**

Van Dyck, Sir Anthony but note l/c *vandyke brown, vandyke beard* etc

various do not use as a pronoun as in "various of the countries protested"; write "several/ many of the countries . . ."

Varsity match acceptable colloquialism for the Oxford-Cambridge rugby match

VAT value-added tax; no longer need to spell out fully

V-chip (electronic scramblers for TV)

VE-Day see **D-Day, VJ-Day**

Velázquez, Diego Rodríguez de Silva y Velázquez (17th-century Spanish artist; not Velasquez); normally last name on its own will suffice

Velcro (cap, proprietary)

veld (not veldt)

ventricles (anatomical; not ventricals)

veranda no final *h*

verbal (pertaining to words); do not confuse with *oral* (pertaining to the mouth). Sadly, corrupted phrases such as *verbal abuse* and *verbal warning* have permeated sports journalism to the point of our having to accept them occasionally, but always try to find an alternative. See **oral**

verbosity watch out for, and eliminate, wordy phrases such as "on the part of" (use *by*), "a large number of" *(many),* "numerous occasions" *(often),* "this day and age" (does not even demand an alternative)

verdict do not use for civil hearings – verdicts come at the end of criminal trials. See **employment tribunals**

verger, virger use the latter in context of St Paul's and Winchester Cathedrals

vermilion (not vermillion)

versus abbreviation is *v* (l/c, no point)

very one of the most overworked words in English. Always try to omit

vetoes plural

viable (capable of independent existence); do not use as a synonym of *feasible* or *practicable*

vicar take care not to use as a generic word for *priest, parson* or *clergyman. Vicar* means specifically the incumbent of a parish (unless a rector); if in doubt, *clergyman* is usually safer. See **Churches** special section (page 172)

vice always hyphenate in its deputy context, eg, *vice-chairman, vice-president* etc but not in its depravity context, eg, *vice squad*. Do not confine the meaning of vice to sex: it is the opposite of virtue and has a correspondingly wide range of meaning

Vice-Chancellor (of a university); cap at first mention, then l/c. See **university posts, job titles**

vice versa roman, no hyphen

Victoria and Albert (Museum); use the ampersand only in the abbreviation *V&A*

videotape one word; but note *video cassette, video recorder/recording. Video* (for film recording) is now common usage and permissible

Vietcong (not Viet Cong)

Virgil (not Vergil)

Virtuality trade name, so cap; do not use as a synonym of *virtual reality*

vis-à-vis note roman, hyphens and accent

viscountcy (describes the rank); see **Titles** special section (page 189)

vitamin A, B, C etc note l/c *v*

viz prefer *namely, that is,* or even *ie*

VJ-Day see **D-Day, VE-Day**

vocal cords (not chords)

voiceover no hyphen

volcanoes plural of volcano

volte-face roman, hyphenated

von (German); usually l/c in the middle of a name, and capped only at the beginning of a sentence. See **Van**

VP never use as abbreviation of *vice-president*

W...

wagon

Wales cap *North Wales, South Wales, Mid Wales, West Wales.* For new counties under the local government reorganisation of 1996, see **unitary authorities**

Walkman trade name, so cap; in general sense, use *personal stereo*

walkout

Wall's (ice-cream etc)

Wan Azizah, wife of Anwar Ibrahim, Malaysian politician. At subsequent mentions, *Dr Azizah* (do not use the Ismail part of her name)

war crimes tribunal cap only when using the full title, *the International War Crimes Tribunal for the Former Yugoslavia.* It sits at The Hague and has a President and a Chief Prosecutor

warfarin not a trade name, so l/c

war game(s) two words

warn transitive verb that requires a direct personal object: ie, a person has to warn somebody about something. Do not write "The Chancellor warned that taxes would rise"; but "The Chancellor *gave warning that/issued a warning that* . . .", or alternatively, "The Chancellor *warned MPs that* . . .". However, we can afford some flexibility in headlines, eg, *Teachers warn of school closures* would be acceptable

wars cap the *First World War, Second World War, Cold War, Korean War, Vietnam War, Gulf War* etc; but prefer the *Falklands conflict* because war was never formally declared; if the phrase has to be used, write *Falklands war* (l/c)

warships take care with the following distinction: to serve *in* a warship, but *on* a merchant ship; a naval officer is *appointed* to serve *in HMS Sheffield,* not *posted* to serve. See **Armed Forces** special section (page 164)

wartime

Washington not usually necessary to add DC (as in Washington DC), but occasionally useful to distinguish it from Washington State (caps). That and New York State are the only two states needing caps to avoid confusion. See **New York**

washout (one word)

waste usually better to write *waste* than *wastage,* which means process of loss, its amount or rate

wastepaper bin/basket

watchdog

watercolour, watercolourist but note *Royal Society of Painters in Water Colours*

Waterstone's (booksellers); note apostrophe

wear write *menswear, women's wear, children's wear, sportswear.* See **clothing**

weather stories (about floods, hurricanes, snow, record sunshine etc in the UK) always take a cross-reference to the back page weather forecast. Style is bold, set right, eg, **Forecast, page 24**

website, but cap **the Web:** see **World Wide Web**

week, weekend the week ends on Saturday night. Common sense will dictate whether to say *last week, this week, next week* etc. Beware of references to *at the weekend* in Monday papers: always make clear whether you mean the weekend just past or next Saturday and Sunday

weights and measures abbreviations context will determine when to abbreviate inches, stone, pounds, ounces etc. "He was 6ft 7in" (not ins, and no space between number and abbreviation); but "she stood two feet from the kerb". Similarly, "she weighed 8st 12lb" (not lbs); but "he was several pounds overweight". See **scientific measures**

weights and measures conversion no longer convert metric measures into their imperial counterpart. See **scientific measures, celsius**

Welch, Welsh note *The Royal Welch Fusiliers,* but *Welsh Guards* (part of The Guards Division). See **Armed Forces** special section (page 164)

welfare state l/c; but note the *Welfare to Work* programme (cap W twice, no hyphens). See **State**

wellbeing

wellington boots note l/c

wellwisher do not hyphenate

Welsh Assembly now capped; and note *First Secretary* (not First Minister) of the Assembly.

Welsh, Irvine (the playwright)

Welsh Valleys for the (former) mining valleys of South Wales

west, western etc for when to cap in geographical context, see **compass points**

West, the (in global political sense); similarly *Western leaders*, *Western Europe* etc

western (as in cowboy films); l/c

whereabouts singular, eg, "his whereabouts is not known". Prefer "nobody knows where he is"

whether rarely needs *or not* to follow it

which see **that**

while (not whilst)

whingeing with middle *e*

whips cap *Chief Whip*, *Whips' Office*, but l/c the unspecific, eg, **a government whip**. See **Politics** special section (page 181)

whisky (from Scotland); *Scotch* is acceptable as alternative; but **whiskey** (from Ireland and America). See **Scotch**

whistle-blower

whistle-stop (tour etc)

Whitbread Round the World Race note caps, no hyphens

White Cliffs of Dover caps

white-collar workers

White Paper note caps, as with *Green Paper*, but cap only those issued by the Government. A "white paper" from the Opposition should be styled in quotes and l/c at first mention, thereafter just l/c. See **Green Paper**, **Politics** special section (page 181)

whiz-kid note only one *z*, but use this colloquialism sparingly

WHO World Health Organisation; spell out at first mention, then *the WHO*

who, whom which of these to use is determined solely by its function in the relative clause. Remember that *whom* has to be the object of the verb in the relative clause. Thus, "she is the woman whom the police wish to interview" (ie, the police wish to interview *her*, not *she*); the other most common use of *whom* is after a preposition such as *by, with* or *from,* eg, "the person from whom he bought a ticket".

Beware of traps, however: "Who do you think did it?" is correct (not *whom*, because *who* is the subject of "did it", not the object of "do you think"); and "Give it to whoever wants it" is correct (not *whomever*) because *whoever* is the subject of the verb *wants*.

Beware too of constructions such as "he squirted ammonia at a van driver who [correct] he believed had cut him up". This is correct because "he believed" is simply an interjection; "who" is not the object of "he believed" but the subject of the subordinate clause, "who … had cut him up"

whodunnit (not whodunit)

why usually superfluous after *reason,* eg, "the reason he did it was …", not "the reason why he did it was …"

wide no hyphen in compounds such as *countrywide, nationwide, worldwide*

wideawake always one word

widow (woman); note *widower* (man); never say "widow of the late John Jones"; she is the "widow of John Jones"

wildfowl, wildlife

Wild West

Wimbledon caps for the *Centre Court, No 1 Court, No 14 Court* etc. See **Sports** special section (page 185)

Winchester College its pupils are *Wykehamists*

wind with strong winds, give a description as well as force number (in numerals), eg, *storm force 10* (add "on the Beaufort scale" where appropriate. The scale grades wind speeds from 0 to 12; Americans use the scale to 17). Never say "gale-force winds" when *gales* is meant

wines l/c in most cases, for both the type and the grape, except where it would look out of place, eg, *bordeaux, burgundy, champagne, claret, moselle, alsace, rioja,* but a *Côtes du Rhône,* a *Hunter Valley chardonnay.* Cap when referring specifically to the wine-growing region, eg, "I prefer a good burgundy to an alsace, but I think the best wines still come from Bordeaux"; "he preferred to buy his champagne only in Champagne"

wine bar two words

Winslet, Kate

Wirral (not Wirrall); permissible to refer to *The Wirral* (cap *T*), but note *the Wirral peninsula*

wistaria (not wisteria)

witch-hunt but note *witchcraft*

withhold (not withold)

witnesses in British courts witnesses go into the witness box and give evidence; they do not take the stand and testify. In the general sense, prefer *witness* to *eyewitness* wherever possible. See **eyewitness**

woebegone, woeful

Wolf Cubs now just Cubs; see **Boy Scouts**

women doctors, women teachers etc adopt the plural through common usage. See **feminine designations, lady**

Woolf reforms several important changes have been made in civil litigation rules and terminology since April 1999. Three of the commonest are: plaintiffs are now *claimants*; a writ is now a *claim form*; and *notices of application* will be served in the place of summonses. For fuller list, see **Courts** special section (page 176)

Woolworths no apostrophe either in formal name for business contexts or colloquial use for the store and products

word-processor, word-processing note hyphens

workers *farmworkers, metalworkers, roadworkers* one word; note two for *car workers, oil workers, office workers* etc

workforce, workshop, work-to-rule

world avoid, wherever possible, phrases such as *the fashion world, the theatre world, the cricket world* etc

World Heritage Site (caps)

World Trade Organisation (successor body to Gatt); abbreviate to WTO; see **Gatt, Uruguay Round**

World Wide Fund for Nature (not Worldwide; nor World Wildlife Fund, its old name); abbreviate to WWF; note the general adjective *worldwide*

World Wide Web (Internet); caps and three words; and *the* Web for short. But keep *website* l/c. See **Internet**

Worrall Thompson, Antony (TV cook)

worthwhile one word; often used where simply *worth* would be better, eg, "the programme was worth recording"

wrack (seaweed or wreckage); do not confuse with *racked by doubts* etc. See **racked**

wreaked (havoc, heavy damage, vengeance etc; not wrought)

write-off noun, similarly the noun *write-up*, but note *a writedown* (in business context)

writes with written-in bylines, prefer the construction "Ann Bloggs writes" to "writes Ann Bloggs". Use the singular with, eg, (Our Foreign Staff writes). Normal style is to use brackets on news and sports pages, italics on features

wrongdoer, wrongdoing but note *wrong-footed, wrong-headed*

WWF abbreviation of the World Wide Fund for Nature and for legal reasons must not be used for the World Wrestling Federation (write *the federation* if a shorter form for the wrestling group is needed). See **World Wide Fund for Nature**

Wyndham's Theatre (London); note the apostrophe

xenophobe, xenophobia

Xerox trade name, so cap

Xhosa (Bantu tribe; not Khosa); note plural Xhosas

Xmas must not be used in *The Times* (unless part of special title or in a direct quote etc)

X-ray now an acceptable abbreviation of *X-ray examination*. Note also the verb *to X-ray someone*. But do not shorten when you mean *an X-ray photograph*

Y...

Yardies (West Indian criminal gangs)

Yarmouth (Isle of Wight); note *Great Yarmouth* on the Norfolk coast

Yellow Pages italics for the book, but roman for the organisation

Yemen (not *the* Yemen)

"yes" vote, "no" vote

yeti (abominable snowman); note l/c

YMCA, YWCA

yoghurt

yoke (oxen); do not confuse with **yolk** (egg)

Yorkshire since the reorganisation of 1996, see **unitary authorities** for how to locate places in the county. Specify the location for smaller towns and villages, eg, Thirsk, North Yorkshire, but not Bradford or Leeds. Note *the Yorkshire Dales*, or simply *the Dales*, and *the North York Moors* (not North Yorkshire Moors)

young offender institution l/c for general use, but cap for specific, eg, *Feltham Young Offender Institution*

Young Turks caps

youth courts not juvenile courts, which no longer exist. See **Courts** special section (page 176)

yuan the Chinese currency (rather than *the renminbi*)

Yugoslav (not Yugoslavian); adjective from Yugoslavia

yuletide (l/c)

yuppie noun or adjective

Yves Saint Laurent (not St)

Z...

Zaire after the overthrow of President Mobutu in May 1997, call the country, at first mention, the Democratic Republic of Congo (formerly Zaire), and thereafter simply Congo. The former French Congo should be called Congo-Brazzaville

Zambezi (not Zambesi)

-ze in almost all cases use the *-ise* ending rather than *-ize*. Two of the main exceptions are *capsize* and *synthesizer*

Zeitgeist (the spirit of the times); note cap and italics

zeppelin (airship); note l/c

Zeta-Jones, Catherine (hyphen)

ziggurat

zigzag, zigzagging

Zimmer frame trademark, so cap

zodiac, zodiacal (as in signs of the zodiac); note l/c

zoo cap as in *London Zoo, Dudley Zoo*; thereafter *the zoo*

THE ARMED FORCES

ROYAL NAVY

At first mention *the Royal Navy* (caps), thereafter *the Navy* (retain the cap); *naval* is l/c except in titles such as *Royal Naval Volunteer Reserve* (RNVR) etc.

Ships are styled *HMS Achilles* or the *Achilles*. They should generally be treated as feminine; thus *she* and *her* rather than *it* and *its*. Ships are *named,* not *christened.* Note that Royal Fleet Auxiliary ships are entitled RFA, eg, *RFA Fort George* (not HMS...)

General terms

alter course (not change)

Armed Forces, Armed Services, the Services caps, but l/c *serviceman, servicewoman.* Also cap *Service* and *Forces* when used adjectivally as in *a Service family*

astern (never behind or following); eg, the *Achilles* was astern of the *Ajax*

Britannia refer to her as the former Royal Yacht

company Royal Navy ships do not have crews, they have ship's company

embarked *in* (not on)

the Fleet cap

line ahead (not astern)

moored or **made fast** (never tied up)

on board preferable to aboard

pennant (not pendant)

ratings (not *other ranks,* in the Navy)

Royal Marines caps

SBS Special Boat Service (no longer Squadron)

serving *in* a warship (but on a merchant ship); an officer is *appointed* to serve *in HMS Sheffield,* not posted to serve . . . Also note that sailors serve *in a submarine,* even though subs are boats

signalman (not signaller)

submarines called *boats* (not ships) in the Royal Navy

tow the towing ship has the towed ship *in* tow; the towed ship is *under* tow

Union Flag (not Union Jack in naval contexts, except when flown at the jackstaff)

under way

weigh anchor (not ship anchor, which would mean that a ship had left her anchor at the bottom of the sea)

Ranks

abbreviation prefer not to abbreviate ranks in text of news stories; however, in lists of promotions etc on the Court Page, the following abbreviations will apply: Adm, Cdre (Commodore), Capt, Cdr (Commander), Lt-Cdr, Lt, CPO (Chief Petty Officer), L/S (Leading Seaman)

hyphenation *Times* style is to hyphenate those ranks consisting of a compound of two individual designations, eg, *Lieutenant-Commander, Commandant-General, Surgeon-Captain*; also any rank with *vice* or *rear*, eg, *Vice-Admiral, Rear-Admiral*. We should also hyphenate *Commander-in-Chief*

flag ranks a flag officer is a rear-admiral or above, exercising command and authorised by the Admiralty to fly a flag. The following are flag ranks: *Admiral of the Fleet, Admiral, Vice-Admiral, Rear-Admiral*. Although the Duke of Edinburgh is an Admiral of the Fleet, the Fleet is actually commanded by an admiral whose job title is *Commander-in-Chief Fleet* (CinC Fleet)

THE ARMY

Cap *the Army* when referred to as *the Service*, eg, "Two hundred new tanks were bought by the Army yesterday", or "He denied that he hated the Army"; but l/c when used adjectivally, eg, "An army raid was launched yesterday on the front line. . . ", or "An army spokesman rejected the idea. . ."

Give soldiers their full title at first mention, eg, General Herbert Carruthers, thereafter General Carruthers or the general. Never refer to them as Mr in news stories.

General terms

beating retreat (not beating the retreat)

guards of honour (ceremonial troops used to greet visiting dignitaries); like all guards, they are *mounted*, as sentries are *posted*

The King's Own Royal Border Regiment (full title)

King's Troop RHA (Royal Horse Artillery), remains thus even though the Sovereign is the Queen

Last Post (not *the*); note it is *sounded* (not played)

parade troops *march* through the streets (not parade)

Royal Corps of Signals may be contracted to *Royal Signals* (not RCS)

Royal Engineers can be abbreviated to RE (not REs)

Royal Electrical and Mechanical Engineers REME for short (never Reme)

The Royal Welch Fusiliers, Welch Regiment but note *Welsh Guards*

SAS Special Air Service (regiment). See **SBS** under **Royal Navy**

Trooping the Colour (not Trooping *of* the Colour)

trumpeters, buglers cavalry regiments have *trumpeters*, infantry regiments have *buglers*. They are not interchangeable

Ranks and regiments

regimental names one of the trickiest areas is when to include *The* as part of the name of regiments. With defence cuts and the amalgamation of regiments in the past few years, titles have changed rapidly, so checking an up-to-date *Army List* is imperative. General styles as follows:

> **Companies** A Company, B Battery, 94 (Locating) Battery, C Squadron

> **Battalions** 1st, 2nd etc, and 1st/5th, 6l Field Regiment, RA

> **Brigades** 24 Infantry Brigade, 5 Airborne Brigade

> **Divisions** 7th Armoured Division

> **Corps** X Corps, XII Corps

> **Armies** First Army

> **Army Groups** 21 Army Group

ranks the same guidance on abbreviation and hyphenation applies as to the Royal Navy (see previous pages):

abbreviation prefer not to abbreviate ranks in text of news stories; however, in lists of promotions etc on the Court Page, the following abbreviations will apply: Gen, Lt-Gen, Maj-Gen, Brig, Col, Lt-Col, Maj, Capt, Lt, 2nd Lt, WO1 (Warrant Officer Class 1), WO2, S Sgt (Staff Sergeant), Sgt, Cpl, Bdr (Bombardier), L Cpl, Pte (Private), Gdsmn (Guardsman), Gnr (Gunner), Rfn (Rifleman)

hyphenation hyphenate those ranks consisting of a compound of two individual designations, eg, *Major-General, Lieutenant-General, Lieutenant-Colonel, Sergeant-Major* etc, but not compounds such as *Staff Sergeant, Lance Corporal*. (Note that *Brigadier-General* does not exist in the British Army, though it does, eg, in the American and French.)

Chief of the Defence Staff a naval Chief of the Defence Staff becomes *Admiral of the Fleet Sir John Jones*; an army one is *Field Marshal Sir John Jones*; and an air force one is *Marshal of the Royal Air Force Sir John Jones*, in each case followed by *Chief of the Defence Staff*

field marshal either a peer or a knight, so at first mention, eg, *Field Marshal Sir Richard Potts*, subsequently *Sir Richard*

officers with personal titles describe in full at first mention, eg, *Lieutenant-General Sir Amos Burke*, subsequently *Sir Amos* or *General Burke*

ROYAL AIR FORCE

Use the *Royal Air Force* or the *RAF* in text, not the Air Force (see **air force** in main section).

Ranks

ranks with ranks, the same guidance on abbreviation applies as to the Royal Navy and the Army (see previous pages)

hyphenation the only RAF rank to take a hyphen is *Air Vice-Marshal*

abbreviations in lists only, as follows: AVM (Air Vice-Marshal), Air Cdre (Air Commodore), Gp Capt (Group Captain), Wg Cdr (Wing Commander), Sqn Ldr (Squadron Leader), Flt Lt (Flight Lieutenant), FO (Flying Officer), PO (Pilot Officer), FS (Flight Sergeant), Chief Tech (Chief Technician), Sgt (Sergeant), Cpl (Corporal), SAC/SACW (Senior

Aircraftman/Senior Aircraftwoman) etc. Note, never shorten Flight Lieutenant to Lieutenant at subsequent mentions.

Types of aircraft (not planes); *Harrier jump-jet*, *Tornado* (plural *Tornados*), *B52*, *F111* (no hyphens), etc

THE ARTS

ART
Titles of paintings, drawings, sculptures and exhibitions are now all in italic.

DANCE
ballets titles in italics

cha-cha-cha (not cha-cha)

Latin dancing cap *L*

pas de deux, corps de ballet roman

paso doble two words

pointe shoes (not point)

FILM
auteur roman

cinéma-vérité roman

8mm film, 16mm etc

films titles in italics

film-maker hyphen

film noir roman

Palme d'or roman

3-D

LITERATURE
Book titles including novels, plays, short stories, poems (short or long), magazine articles, chapter headings, textbooks, reference books, biographies etc take italics. But do not italicise the Bible, the Talmud, the Koran, Book of Genesis etc.

MUSIC

Song titles (classical or pop) take italics; no need to cap every word in the title, eg, *Bring it on Home to Me* rather than *Bring It On Home To Me.*

albums titles in italics

First Violin Concerto note roman and caps, because it is a genre

Mozart works use the numbering system of Köchel, eg, K527

Number abbreviate to No, eg, Symphony No 3

operas titles in italics, as arias

Opus write, eg, Op (Op28)

orchestral works those with non-genre titles take italics, eg, *Night on the Bare Mountain*

Proms, the no need to spell out Promenade Concerts; note also caps for *Promenaders*; *the Last Night of the Proms*

Requiem roman caps, because it is a genre

symphony style is roman caps, eg, Symphony No 3; but where symphonies have numbers and popular alternative titles, place the title in italics, eg, *Eroica*. Spell out ordinals, eg, Mahler's Fourth Symphony, but note Symphony No 4

tempos (not tempi)

virtuosos (not virtuosi)

THEATRE

Act I, scene 2 etc cap Act and use Roman numeral, l/c scene and Arabic numeral

dramatis personae roman

plays titles in italics

Wyndham's Theatre (London)

TV AND RADIO

Television and radio programmes take italics, except for first mention in reviews, when they go in bold.

GENERAL ARTS TERMS

a cappella

Albert Hall, Festival Hall, National Theatre generally omit *Royal*; but note *Royal Opera House, Royal Shakespeare Company, Royal Ballet* (which is different from the *Birmingham Royal Ballet*), etc

Arts Council thereafter l/c *the council* provided the context is clear

Bartók, Béla

the Beatles, the Rolling Stones etc no need to cap *the* unless at the start of a sentence; but prefer to keep cap *T* with *The Who* and *The The*

cinemagoer, dancegoer, theatregoer one word

commedia dell'arte

debut, decor, matinee, premiere note no accents

Dvořák, Antonin

hi-fi

Internet, the note cap; also *the Net, World Wide Web, the Web,* but lower case for *website*

Janáček, Leos

Janet Holmes à Court

mezzo-soprano hyphen

nightclub

subplot, subtext, subtitle

Symphony Hall, Birmingham omit *the*

3-D

THE CHURCHES

GENERAL STYLES

Anglican bishops note they are *consecrated*; Roman Catholic bishops are *ordained*

Archbishop of Canterbury is Primate of All England; note the *Archbishop of York* is Primate of England

biblical references write, eg, II Corinthians ii, 2; Luke iv, 5

Bible, the always cap and roman, similarly the Koran, the Talmud; but note l/c *biblical*. Also caps and roman for Books of the Bible, eg, Book of Job

caps or **l/c** use caps for Bible (note l/c *biblical*), Blessed Sacrament, (Holy) Communion, the Cross, the Crucifixion, Eucharist, the Gospels, (Requiem) Mass, the Resurrection etc; use l/c for baptism, confirmation, evensong, last rites, matins, ordination, psalms (but the *Book of Psalms*)

churches use caps with, eg, the Church of England, the Roman Catholic Church, the United Reformed Church, the Methodist Church, the Church Army. Also cap the Church in context of the institution (but not adjectivally, as in "the vicar accused church authorities yesterday . . ."). For individual churches, write, eg, St James's Church, Bighampton, or simply St James's, Bighampton

Church Commissioners cap first mention, then l/c *the commissioners*; note there are three chief officers: the First (Second, Third) Church Estates Commissioner

churchgoer one word

Church of Ireland, Church in Wales (NB *in*), **Scottish Episcopal Church** note that these are Anglican but disestablished; the *Church of Scotland* is Presbyterian but established

Episcopal(ian) means Anglican in the United States, Scotland and elsewhere

General Synod cap at first mention, thereafter l/c *the synod*. It has three houses: bishops, clergy and laity

hymns names go in italics

Nonconformist and **Free Churches** caps; note that the *United Reformed*

Church is composed of the former Congregational Church and the Presbyterian Church of England; but some "Congregational" congregations remain outside the reformed group

Pope, the not usually necessary to give his full name, eg, Pope John Paul II (unless several Popes are mentioned in a story), but always cap. Note l/c *papacy, pontiff*

Rev never ever write the solecism the Rev Brown or (even worse) Rev Brown. The correct style is *the Rev Joseph Brown*, thereafter *Mr Brown*

Roman Catholic at first mention in full; thereafter *Catholic* is acceptable

Scotland distinguish the *Free Church of Scotland* (the "Wee Frees") from the established *Church of Scotland* and also from the *Presbyterian Church of Scotland*, of which Lord Mackay of Clashfern is a member. Note the *Moderator of the General Assembly of the Church of Scotland* (not Moderator of the Church of Scotland)

Supreme Governor of the Church of England (the Queen; note not *head* of the Church of England)

Trinity note cap pronoun, eg, *Jesus's teachings, His example; God is He*

Vicar do not use as a generic word for *priest, parson, clergyman* etc. Vicar means specifically the incumbent of a parish (unless a rector). If in doubt, *clergyman* is usually a safer term

TITLES
Senior clergy, Anglicans

bishops and **archbishops** by convention, always follow the title of their office, eg, the Archbishop of Canterbury, Dr George Carey; the Archbishop of Barchester, the Most Rev John Smith; or (for diocesan bishops), the Bishop of Barchester, the Right Rev John Smith. Use Dr when appropriate, though not all high ecclesiastics have doctorates; eg, the Bishop of Lowchester, Dr John Smith; subsequent references, the archbishop (bishop), or Dr Smith (if so entitled) – never Mr Smith

archdeacons below archbishops and bishops, similar styles prevail, eg, Archdeacon of Barchester, the Ven John Smith (thereafter Mr Smith or, more commonly, Canon Smith)

cathedral deans and provosts write, eg, the Dean of Barchester, the

Very Rev John Smith (Dean Smith)

rural deans just the Rev John Smith (Mr Smith)

canons and prebendaries write, eg, Canon/Prebendary John Smith, thereafter Canon Smith

Senior clergy, Roman Catholic

archbishops at first mention, the Roman Catholic Archbishop of Liverpool, the Most Rev Patrick Kelly; subsequent mention Archbishop Kelly or the archbishop

Archbishop of Westminster, Cardinal X – no need to say Roman Catholic Archbishop of Westminster, but note Roman Catholic Archdiocese of Westminster. Subsequent mentions, Cardinal X

bishops first mention the Roman Catholic Bishop of Plymouth, the Right Rev Christopher Budd, thereafter Bishop Budd or the bishop; very few Catholic archbishops or bishops have doctorates, but if so, write, eg, Dr Budd

Monsignor (abbreviate to Mgr); do not use for Roman Catholic archbishops or bishops in Britain, though it can be a convenient form in foreign stories

Junior clergy

Christian priests, deacons, ministers, rectors, vicars of all denominations except Roman Catholic or Orthodox write, eg, the Rev Frank Faith at first mention, thereafter Mr Faith (see General Styles, under Rev). For *women clergy*, write the Rev Joan Faith, thereafter Mrs Faith or Miss Faith

Roman Catholic and Orthodox clergy write, eg, Father Justin Hope at first mention (avoid the ugly Fr abbreviation), thereafter Father Hope for Catholics, but Father Justin for Orthodox. Also use Father with Benedictines, eg, Father Goode, not Dom Goode

nuns use Sister Charity, Mother Charity, Mother Teresa

Jesuits take designation SJ on first mention, eg, "the Rev Albert Leader, SJ, said yesterday . . ."

Foreign prelates

Ireland, Africa, North America etc write Anglican Bishop of . . ., Roman Catholic Bishop of . . .; but in countries where, for example, Roman Catholicism is the overwhelming faith, the denomination may be superfluous (eg, the Archbishop of Warsaw ...) or supplied by context

South Africa

Church of the Province of Southern Africa (or Church of the Province, or the Anglican Church) is Anglican but sometimes uses incense, Stations of the Cross etc

The Church of England (in South Africa); separate entity from the Anglican Church. The Church of England split from the Anglican communion in the late 19th century; incense, Stations of the Cross etc are not used

THE COURTS

civil cases These are heard in magistrates' courts and county courts, the more serious in the High Court, which has three divisions – the Queen's Bench, Chancery, and Family Divisions (cap Division in full title). In London they are based at the Royal Courts of Justice in the Strand.

The Divisional Court of the Queen's Bench Division can quash decisions by magistrates' courts and hear appeals from lower courts on points of law. It is also the court for reviewing governmental bodies' or local authorities' decisions – judicial review. Distinguish between applications for leave and the main hearing

criminal cases Most of these are dealt with by magistrates' courts, presided over by magistrates, who are lay justices (JPs). The busiest have full-time paid magistrates, stipendiaries. The more serious criminal cases are heard in the Crown Court, of which the most famous (in the City of London) is the Central Criminal Court, or Old Bailey (either form acceptable)

Court of Appeal always use the full title at first mention and wherever possible thereafter, though *appeal court* (l/c) may be used sparingly. The court sits with three judges, who are Lords Justices of Appeal. The highest court in the land is the Judicial Committee of the House of Lords (though normally the *House of Lords* or simply l/c *the law lords* will suffice); they are the most senior judges, formally called the Lords of Appeal in Ordinary

Scottish courts Court of Session, Edinburgh (for civil actions); High Court of Justiciary (prosecution of serious crimes and criminal appeals); the senior judge is Lord President (of the Court of Session) and also Lord Justice-General (in High Court); others are Lord Justice-Clerk (in both) and, formally, Lords of Session and Lords Commissioners of Justiciary. Sheriff (not sheriff's) Courts deal with less serious criminal and civil cases. Other points in Scotland: advocate (equivalent of English barrister); the Crown prosecutors are the Lord Advocate and Advocates-Depute and (in each sheriffdom) the Procurator Fiscal (plural, Procurators Fiscal); in civil actions, pursuer (equivalent of plaintiff), defender (the defendant), summons (writ containing pursuer's case)

youth courts these have replaced the old juvenile courts

JUDGES

bench, the (in magistrates' courts) always l/c

circuit judge sits either in the Crown Court or in the county court and should be referred to as Judge Joe Bean, QC, (the QC where appropriate). Circuit judges may also sit in the High Court, in which case they should be described as "Judge Joe Bean, sitting as a High Court judge..."

Court of Appeal judges are Lords Justices of Appeal. Use Lord Justice Bean throughout, or out of court context, Sir John Bean. Note Lady Justice Butler-Sloss. Also Lord Justice Brooke (not Brook)

district judge replaced the old county court registrar and is referred to (at first mention) as District Judge Fred Brown

High Court judges should be referred to as Mr (or Mrs) Justice Bean throughout. First names are not normally necessary unless there are two or more High Court judges with the same surname, where it is essential to differentiate. These judges have a knighthood and may also be described as Sir John Bean, Dame Eleanor Bean etc, but generally only out of the court context. It is correct, however, to refer judicially to Sir Richard Scott, Vice-Chancellor of the Supreme Court, and Sir Stephen Brown, President of the Family Division

House of Lords, or **law lords** the most senior judges, they are the Lords of Appeal in Ordinary. Call them Lord Bean, in or out of court; first mention, give full title, eg, Lord Bean of Muckleflugga, thereafter Lord Bean. When writing about their judgments, say "the House of Lords ruled" or "the law lords ruled"

recorder at the Central Criminal Court, the Recorder of the City of London is usually referred to as "the Recorder". Note caps for the Common Serjeant. The Recorder of London, Recorder of Liverpool and Recorder of Manchester (and no other places) are *circuit judges* and are referred to at first mention as Judge Michael Bean, Recorder of Manchester etc (thereafter the recorder, not Mr Recorder)

retired judges refer to retired judges as follows:

retired High Court judges Sir Ivan Parsons
retired Crown Court judges George Vickers, QC, (first mention), then Mr Vickers

COURT REPORTING

appeals in criminal cases, the defendant becomes the appellant; the respondent is usually the Crown. Say "counsel for Mr Smith" rather than "counsel for the appellant". In civil appeals, either the claimant (plaintiff) or the defendant can be the appellant; it is always better to identify the parties and then avoid the phrase *counsel for the appellant/respondent* wherever possible

caps for courts cap when specific, eg Birmingham Crown Court, Clerkenwell County Court, Dawlish Magistrates' Court, Ashford Youth Court etc; in a general, unspecific context, always cap the High Court, and the Crown Court (it sits in about 90 centres); but l/c county court, magistrates' court, youth court etc

civil cases the parties in civil cases are *the claimant* (formerly the plaintiff) and *the defendant*. Write "counsel for Mrs Y" rather than "counsel for the claimant" etc. In judicial review, the person challenging the decision is *the applicant*

commercial court l/c, as not an official division of the High Court (unlike the Family Division, Queen's Bench Division etc)

coroner's court at inquests, the coroner is l/c unless specific, as in the Westminster Coroner. Juries *return* the verdict, the coroner *records* it. Be careful not to describe pathologists automatically as a Home Office pathologist – most are private consultants, so always check and use simply "the pathologist" if in doubt. There are no coroner's inquests in Scotland: sudden deaths are reported to the Procurator Fiscal, who may hold a fatal accident inquiry

Criminal Bar (caps); similarly, the *Commercial Bar* etc

criminal cases lawyers here appear "for the prosecution", "for the defence" (avoid "prosecuting", "defending"). To *admit* or *deny an offence* is preferred to "pleads guilty" or "pleads not guilty", though the latter form is not banned.

Do not report details of sex offences involving children and do not allow sex trial reports to become surreptitious pornography. Also, do not identify victims of alleged sexual offences.

At the end of a court report, say if the trial – or the hearing, in a civil case – continues. Always give the verdict at the end of a trial or hearing.

Defendants take their titles Mr, Mrs etc until they are convicted (see **appellations**, paragraph f)

Director of Public Prosecutions heads the Crown Prosecution Service

(CPS), whose lawyers are Crown prosecutors; abbreviate to DPP

Inns of Court order of precedence is Lincoln's Inn, Inner Temple, Middle Temple, Gray's Inn

Latin phrases go in roman, eg, mandamus, habeas corpus, certiorari etc, but maxims take italic, eg, *caveat emptor*

Law Report cases cited go in italics, eg, *Gornall v Ritter* and in *Gornall's* case. In news reports and features, use roman

legal bodies or services (from 1999): *Legal Services Commission*; *Community Legal Service*; *Criminal Defence Service* (all caps)

legal officers cap Official Solicitor, Treasury Solicitor, Senior Official Receiver; but note l/c *official receiver*, because there are several. These should be distinguished from the *law officers*, who are *the Attorney-General* and *the Solicitor-General*

"no win, no fee" legislation/agreement etc

Office for the Supervision of Solicitors (no longer the Solicitors Complaints Bureau)

President of the Law Society and **Chairman of the Bar Council** note now capped

prosecution, defence note *Times* style in court reports is *for the prosecution* and *for the defence* (not *prosecuting* and *defending)*

recorders when part-time judges, barristers or solicitors are sitting as recorders, refer to them as, eg, Donald Williams, QC, (where appropriate) the Recorder (later mentions, Mr Williams or the recorder); never write Mr Recorder Williams etc

silk barristers *take silk* and *become silks*; note l/c

small claims court l/c, as not its official title

solicitors never refer to a "company" of solicitors – they are always "firms". Always omit Messrs before the firm's name, eg, simply Sue, Grabbit & Run

titles in general, use l/c for titles etc except when in full or specific; thus, Anthony Bloggs, QC, the Recorder (thereafter the recorder), the West London Magistrate, Chelmsford Crown Court, Horseferry Road Magistrates' Court, Dawlish Magistrates' Court (caps on first mention), etc; but "the court was told", "the judge said", "the magistrate ordered" etc. *The Bench* is capped only when referring to the judges as a group; *a bench of magistrates* is always l/c. Always cap *the Bar* and *the Inn* (even when used on its own)

Woolf reforms In April 1999 new procedural rules for the conduct of civil litigation came into force, including important changes of terminology. These include:

a plaintiff is now a *claimant*

a writ is now a *claim form*

all pleadings are *statements of case*

affidavits become very rare; most written evidence will simply be verified by a *statement of truth*

notices of application will be served in the place of summonses

The means by which justice will be speeded up and administered is *allocation* to the appropriate track; the *small claims track* (up to £5,000), the *fast track* (up to £15,000), and the *multitrack* (the rest)

INTERNATIONAL COURTS

Court of Auditors sits in Luxembourg. It is the fifth institution of the EU, under the Maastricht treaty. (The others are the Council of the European Union, the European Commission, the European Court of Justice and the European Parliament.)

European Court of Human Rights sits in Strasbourg. It is the judicial body of the Council of Europe (not an EC or EU body); the human rights court rules on cases brought against states under the Convention for the Protection of Human Rights and Fundamental Freedoms, usually referred to as the **European Convention on Human Rights**. From November 1998, the European Court of Human Rights has incorporated the former European Commission of Human Rights.

In the Strasbourg context note that neither the Parliamentary Assembly of the Council of Europe nor the Committee of Ministers of the Council of Europe is an EU institution

European Court of Justice sits in Luxembourg. It is the shortened (and usual) form of the Court of Justice of the European Communities. The *Advocate General* (caps, no hyphen) sits in the European Court; he presents the case to the court and delivers an opinion, then the court makes its judgment

International Court of Justice sits in The Hague. It is the judicial organ of the UN and only states can be parties there

POLITICS

GENERAL POINTS

Always check the spelling of MPs and their constituencies if not entirely familiar: the best reference is *The Times Guide to the House of Commons*. Similarly, check *Vacher's Parliamentary Companion* or *Who's Who* for peers.

For guidance on when to cap or l/c Government, Opposition, Parliament, Party, see individual entries in the main section of this Style Guide.

Government, Cabinet, Opposition, Parliament, Party etc take the singular verb, eg, the Cabinet is considering ...

It is never necessary to say *Tony Blair, the Prime Minister,* etc: we may assume that *Times* readers know who the Prime Minister is. But it may be helpful to the flow of the story to write, eg, *the Prime Minister said* ... lower down the story, to avoid the endless repetition of *Mr Blair.*

PARLIAMENTARY TERMS

Act(s) always cap, whether fully identified or not

backbench, frontbench (adjective); similarly *backbenchers, frontbenchers, crossbench* (in the Lords); but note *the back benches, the front bench* and *the cross benches*

Bill(s) always cap (as with Acts above). Bills are read a first time without a debate. The second reading debate is the debate on the principle of the Bill. The Bill then goes to its committee stage, usually in a standing committee composed of about 20 MPs, but occasionally on the floor of the Commons. It then returns to the Commons chamber for its report stage and third reading, which is the final debate on the principle of the Bill. It then goes to the Lords, where similar procedures apply. Note that some legislation starts in the Lords and comes to the Commons thereafter

Cabinet always cap (as with Act and Bill), whether used as a noun or adjectivally, except in the informal *kitchen cabinet. Cabinet committees* should be capped

chamber l/c

Clause Four (as in Labour Party policy); but *Clause 4* permissible in headlines

closure as in *move the closure*

committees cap select committees when full title, such as the Select Committee on the Environment; Cabinet committees such as the Cabinet Committee on the Intelligence Services; the *Public Accounts Committee* (PAC); the *1922 Committee* (of Tory backbenchers); the *National Executive Committee* (NEC) of the Labour Party (or *Labour's national executive* as a shorter alternative)

crossbench, the cross benches see **backbench**

Cunningham through common usage, refer to him at first mention as Jack Cunningham (rather than John), then Dr Cunningham (though he is not a medical doctor)

deputy speakers there are three, and should appear thus: John Jones, the Deputy Speaker

dispatch box l/c

Downing Street policy unit; 10 Downing Street, or **No 10**

Duncan Smith, Iain no hyphen

early day motion l/c

elections always l/c *general election*; similarly *by-election, European elections* etc

frontbench (adjective); note *the front bench*; see **backbench**

galleries l/c, but note the *Press Gallery, Strangers' Gallery* etc

group cap in cases such as the *92 Group* (of Tory rightwingers)

guillotine l/c, no quotation marks

Hamilton, Sir Archibald (not Sir Archie)

Hansard italics

House of Lords officers note *the Clerk of the Parliaments, the Clerk Assistant* (of the Parliaments), *the Reading Clerk* (of the House of Lords)

leaders cap the *Leader of the House, Leader of the Opposition*, but l/c for *the Conservative/Labour/Liberal Democrat leader, the leader of the party* etc

Liberal Democrats permissible to use *Lib Dems* in either headlines or text (though sparingly in text). The term *Liberals* must not be used as a synonym of Liberal Democrats

Lower House caps

Members of Parliament note caps; in almost every case, MPs is the preferable form. But in the Political Sketch, and discursive or commentary articles, the term *Members* sometimes occurs for stylistic reasons and should be retained and capped; similarly in such articles, the Member for Billericay, the Hon Member etc

National Executive Committee of the Labour Party, or simply *Labour's national executive*; abbreviate to NEC

new Labour (as in Tony Blair's policies); l/c *n*, quotes not usually necessary, except when the writer or speaker is making a particular, perhaps ironic, point. But keep caps in slogans such as "New Labour, New Danger"; note *New Deal*

1922 Committee (of Tory backbenchers)

One Nation Tories, One Nation politics etc

Opposition the same cap or l/c rules apply as to Government, ie, cap as a noun but generally l/c as an adjective, eg, "He accused the Opposition of lying", but "He said it was an opposition lie"

order, order paper l/c

Parliament cap always in the British context (for when to cap foreign parliaments, see **Parliament** in main section). The cap rule now applies even to phrases such as *the lifetime of this Parliament* or *the Bill is unlikely to progress until the next Parliament*. The adjective *parliamentary* is usually l/c except when used as part of a title, eg, *Parliamentary Labour Party* (PLP)

parliamentary private secretary l/c, abbreviate to PPS

Part I, Part II (of Bill etc); caps also for *Section 2*, *Article 8* etc

party abbreviations in lists or political sketches or reports of debates where party affiliation is added after an MP's name – eg, Tony Benn (Lab, Chesterfield) – use *Lab* for Labour, *C* for Conservative (not Con), and *LD* for Liberal Democrat (not Lib Dem)

party conferences l/c, as in *Labour Party conference*

Private Member's Bill caps

Public Accounts Committee abbreviate to PAC

Queen's Speech caps

Question Time, Prime Minister's Questions also *Agriculture Questions, Treasury Questions* etc; but note l/c *questions* to the Prime Minister, the Foreign Secretary etc

Register of Members' Interests caps

Royal Assent caps

royal commissions see main section

select committees cap when giving full title, eg, *Treasury Select Committee*

Serjeant at Arms

Smith the widow of John Smith is Baroness Smith of Gilmorehill, thereafter Lady Smith; she is not Dame Elizabeth Smith

Speaker usual style is Betty Boothroyd, the Speaker, at first mention, thereafter the Speaker or Miss Boothroyd

spin-doctor hyphen

State Opening (of Parliament); note caps

ten-minute rule (Bill etc)

Treasury bench

Upper House caps

Vote (of money); takes cap

whips cap for the *Chief Whip, Opposition Chief Whip, Whips' Office*; but l/c as in *three-line whip, to lose the party whip, a government whip*

SPORTS

Sports writing is notoriously vulnerable to cliché and jargon. Apart from direct quotes, avoid the type of language used by players and TV commentators.

GENERAL STYLES

All England Club

baseball inning (not innings)

Blue (from Oxford, Cambridge, for the award or the sportsman or woman); note cap

cross country hyphenate only in adjectival use, as in *cross-country trials*

Cup Final cap *the FA Cup Final*, but note l/c *f* for *World Cup final*, *Worthington Cup final*, *Benson and Hedges Cup final* etc; also l/c for *FA Cup semi-final*, because by definition more than one

divisions, groups, sections etc in sporting context these always take l/c, eg, *World Cup group A*, *Nationwide League first division*, *European championship section D* etc

England Under-21 etc

first division, second division etc (not Division One, 2, etc or any variant)

hat-trick (cricket or football)

racecourse, racehorse but note *horse race, horse racing*

stretchered off avoid; instead use *carried off on a stretcher*

women's competitions, championships, events etc (not ladies')

World Cup caps; note l/c for *world championship* in all sports

BOXING

General terms featherweight, heavyweight, light-heavyweight etc; knockout(s)

CRICKET

General terms wicketkeeper, mid-off, mid-wicket; follow on (verb) but the follow-on; hat-trick; hit-wicket; mis-hit; third man; extra cover; off break; leg-before; no-ball; a four (not 4); AXA Life League; Benson and Hedges Cup

delivery in cricket this is a bowling action, not a ball, eg, "Qadir has a puzzling delivery", not "Warne bowled Gatting with his first delivery"

England and Wales Cricket Board from January 1, 1997, the ECB took control of all levels of the domestic game, and the Test and County Cricket Board (TCCB) is no more

First-Class Forum represents the views of the first-class counties; abbreviate to FCF

MCC Marylebone Cricket Club; concerned with the laws of cricket and matters at Lord's. Do not refer to *the* MCC

off spinner (bowler who bowls off breaks)

FOOTBALL

By itself, football means the association code. *Soccer* is now an acceptable alternative.

American football should always be described thus, unless the context is so obvious that football on its own is enough.

General terms goalkeeper, kick-off (noun), Arsenal (not *the*), midfield, offside

Fifa (football's governing body; not FIFA); similarly *Uefa* (not UEFA)

Football Association, or **FA** (never the English Football Association)

FA Carling Premiership at first mention write in full, thereafter *the Premiership*. Do not confuse with the *FA Premier League*

FA Premier League (organisation that runs the FA Carling Premiership); take care not to confuse the competition and the organisation

Nationwide League first division, second division etc (lower divisions; no longer Endsleigh); note l/c. This competition is run by the *Football League*

St Andrew's, Birmingham; do not confuse with St Andrews (golf)

St James' Park, Newcastle and Exeter

RUGBY UNION, RUGBY LEAGUE

General terms full back; scrum half; fly half; dropped goal; knock on (verb) but a knock-on (noun); scrummage; threequarter; open-side flanker; wing (not winger); lineout(s); 22-metre line, the 22; touch judge; triple crown; grand slam; the British Isles, not the British Lions (though Lions on its own is acceptable at second mention)
Note stand-off half in rugby league

rugby union, **rugby league** both take l/c in general usage (though not, of course, in titles)

rugger do not use

Six Nations Championship note caps, and no longer Five Nations except in historical contexts

GOLF

The holes should appear in both text and results as 1st, 2nd, 10th, 18th, but write the "third extra hole" after that. In a match-play use, "Jones beat Brown 2 and 1" (not two and one). Usual *Times* style for numbers (spell out from one to ten, figures thereafter) in sentences such as "Faldo holed from eight feet/15 feet".

General terms the Open Championship (not British Open); bogey; birdie; eagle (no quotes); dormy, only if the match can be halved (a player cannot be dormy if the match can be taken to, say, the 19th hole to reach a decision)

MOTOR RACING

British Grand Prix, Japanese Grand Prix etc cap as specific; but note l/c for unspecific *grand prix racing* etc ; plural *grands prix*

Formula One motor racing two caps; spell out *One*

pitstop (one word)

SWIMMING

General terms freestyle, backstroke, breaststroke (no hyphens)

TENNIS

Flushing Meadows, New York (home of the US Open tennis

championships; not Meadow)

Moyà, Carlos note accent

YACHTING

America's Cup

sailing correspondent (not yachting correspondent)

Whitbread Round the World Race caps, no hyphens

TITLES

ROYAL FAMILY

Diana, Princess of Wales, at first mention; though since her death use the form *the late Princess* where appropriate. Never refer to her as Princess Diana or (even worse) Lady Di or Princess Di. Also, note one comma only for the *Diana, Princess of Wales Memorial Fund*

Duke of Edinburgh, the thereafter *the Duke* or (sparingly) *Prince Philip*

Duke of York, the thereafter *the Duke* or *Prince Andrew*. Note the *Duchess of York* is no longer a member of the Royal Family since her divorce. At first mention, refer to her as *the Duchess of York*, then l/c *the duchess* – never "Fergie" or any such vulgarity

Earl of Wessex, the thereafter *the Earl* or *Prince Edward*; similarly the *Countess of Wessex, the Countess,* or t*he former Sophie Rhys-Jones*

Prince of Wales, the thereafter *the Prince* or (sparingly) *Prince Charles*

Princess Royal, the thereafter *the Princess*. Use *Princess Anne* only in historical context

Queen, the try to use *the* even in headlines

Queen Elizabeth the Queen Mother (no comma) first mention, thereafter the Queen Mother

Royal Dukes keep the cap at subsequent mentions (eg, the *Duke of Kent*, later *the Duke*); other dukes do not retain the cap (see below)

PEERAGE AND KNIGHTS

Titles of nobility in descending order as follows: *duke, marquess* (not marquis, except in foreign contexts and occasional Scottish titles), *earl, viscount* and *baron*. At first mention, give the formal title (as in *Who's Who*) eg, the Marquess of Paddington, the Earl of Waterloo, but then Lord Paddington, Lord Waterloo etc. This does not apply to *barons*, who are always Lord except in the announcement of new baronies. *Dukes* are always dukes and do not become Lord (eg, the Duke of Rutland). Note style of *the 2nd Earl, the 3rd Viscount* etc. Note a major difference from royalty is that these titles take l/c rather than cap after the first mention, (eg, the Duke of Argyll, thereafter the duke).

announcement of titles baronets, knights and dames take the appropriate title as soon as the honour is announced. Peers have to submit their choice of title for approval, so wait until the formal public announcement (usually in *The London Gazette*)

baron always Lord except in the announcement of new baronies

baronesses in their own right or life peeresses are *Baroness* at first mention, and then *Lady* (eg, Baroness Thatcher, then Lady Thatcher)

baronets, knights write, eg, Sir John Euston, thereafter Sir John. Note the wife of a baronet is called Lady from the start, eg, Lady Euston. Remember this essential point: no wife of a baronet or knight takes her first name in her title unless she is the daughter of a duke, a marquess or an earl. If a baronet has had more than one wife, the first wife is, eg, Mary Lady Smith (no commas) – the same form applies to the widow of a baron. If a knight has had more than one wife, the former wife puts her Christian name in brackets, eg, Lady (Alice) Brown, to distinguish her from the present wife, Lady Brown.

If two baronets or knights have the same name, their wives (when mentioned apart from their husbands) put his first name in brackets, eg, Lady (Stephen) Brown, Lady (Andrew) Brown

children of peers eldest son**s** of a duke, marquess or earl use the father's second title as a courtesy title (eg, the Duke of Bedford's son is the Marquess of Tavistock). These people are not peers, even in headlines. Younger sons of dukes and marquesses use their first names and the family surname (eg, Lord John Worthington; subsequent mention Lord John, never Lord Worthington; his wife is Lady John Worthington).

Daughters of dukes, marquesses or earls take their first names in their title, eg, Lady Olive York, and in subsequent mentions Lady Olive (never Lady York).

Younger sons of earls and all children of viscounts and barons have the style *the Hon,* but use this only in Court Page copy; normally, they are simply Mr, Miss, Ms etc (none is a peer)

countess (wife of an earl); use *Lady* at subsequent mentions

Dames (of an order of chivalry); dames take the same style as knights, eg, Dame Felicity Brown, thereafter Dame Felicity. A dame who is married may prefer to use her own style, eg, Dame Jennifer Jenkins, wife of Lord Jenkins of Hillhead; personal preferences should be respected

duchess (wife of a duke) always *Duchess*, eg, the Duchess of X

duke always described as duke so does not become Lord at subsequent mention. The wife of a duke is a *duchess*

earl at first mention, give the formal title, thereafter Lord. The wife of an earl is a *countess*

first names with titles take great care especially with the names of wives of peers, baronets and knights. No wife of a baronet or knight takes her first name in her title unless she is the daughter of a duke, a marquess or an earl. The wife of Lord St Pancras is simply Lady St Pancras. The wife of Sir John Fenchurch is simply Lady Fenchurch (together, Sir John and Lady Fenchurch). However, when the name is a common one and there is no other convenient identification, or where there is some other compelling reason, it is permissible to say Lady (John) Brown (brackets essential; see **baronets, knights**)

marchioness (wife of a marquess); use *Lady* at subsequent mentions

marquess (not marquis, except in foreign contexts and occasional Scottish titles). At first mention, give the formal title and thereafter Lord. The wife of a marquess is a *marchioness*

titles including place name some titles include a place name, eg, Lord Callaghan of Cardiff, Lord Archer of Weston-super-Mare, while others do not. Follow *Who's Who*, where those whose place name must be included appear in **bold caps.**

Always give the full title at first mention, thereafter the abbreviated form, eg, Lord Bingham of Cornhill, thereafter Lord Bingham. Among titles spelt differently from the place name are the Marquess of Ailesbury, Marquess of Donegall, Earl of Guilford, Earl of Scarbrough

viscount give formal title at first mention, thereafter Lord. The wife of a viscount is a *viscountess*

viscountess (wife of a viscount); give full title, then *Lady* at subsequent mentions

widows/former wives of titles those who have not remarried use their first name before the title, eg, Margaret Duchess of Argyll (no commas). A widow may also be known as the Dowager Duchess of Y, or the Dowager Lady Z